GLOBAL MARKET STRATEGIES

A useful suggestion How the Fastest-Growing Companies in the World Expand Their Businesses Across Borders to Avoid Failure Concentrating locally or globally

RICHARD N. WILLIAMS

All right reserved. No part of this publication may be reproduced, distributed or transmitted in any form or by any means including photocopy, recording or other electronic or mechanical methods, without the prior written permission of the publisher, except in the case of brief quotations embodied in critical reviews and certain other noncommercial uses permitted by copyright law.
Copyright Richard N. Williams

TABLE OF CONTENTS

Overview of Global Market Expansion 3
Importance of Going Beyond Borders 3
Chapter 1 3
Market Research and Analysis 3
Conducting Global Market Research 3
Analyzing Target Markets and Competitors 3
Chapter 2 3
Legal and Regulatory Considerations 3
Understanding International Business Laws 3
Navigating Trade Regulations and Compliance 3
Chapter 3 3
Cultural and Linguistic Challenges 3
Adapting to Cultural Differences 3
Overcoming Language Barriers in Global Business 3
Chapter 4 3
Market Entry Strategies 3
Choosing the Right Entry Mode 3
Joint Ventures, Partnerships, and Acquisitions 3
Chapter 5 3
Global Marketing and Branding 3
Crafting a Global Marketing Strategy 3
Building a Consistent Global Brand Image 3
Chapter 6 3
Supply Chain and Logistics 3
Managing International Supply Chains 3
Efficient Global Logistics Planning 3
Chapter 9 3
Financial Planning and Risk Management 3
Budgeting for Global Expansion 3
Mitigating Financial Risks in International Markets 3
Chapter 10 Technology and Digital Presence 3
Leveraging Technology for Global Reach 3
Establishing a Strong Online Presence 3

Chapter 11 3
Case Studies 3
Real-world Examples of Successful Global Market Expansion 3
CONCLUSION 3
Key Strategies on Looking Ahead to Future Global Business Trends
.... 3
INTRODUCTION 1

INTRODUCTION

In the clamoring city of New York, Alex Turner, a carefully prepared business visionary, ended up at a junction. His fruitful neighborhood business had arrived at a level, and he longed for development past lines. Not entirely set in stone to leave on an excursion of worldwide development, Alex dug into the domain of worldwide market methodologies.

Driven by a versatile soul, Alex previously submerged himself in figuring out the complexities of global business sectors. Late evenings were spent poring over market patterns, social subtleties, and monetary scenes. He contacted industry specialists, encouraging associations that would later demonstrate priceless. This period of fastidious exploration established the groundwork for his creative way to deal with business extension.

Equipped with bits of knowledge, Alex concocted a far reaching worldwide market section procedure. Rather than quickly bouncing into unfamiliar business sectors, he decided to steer his items in areas with comparative social affinities. This essential move permitted him to adjust his contributions to nearby inclinations while limiting dangers related with new business sectors.

Alex's inventive change was not restricted to item transformation. He embraced innovation to associate with potential clients around the world. Utilizing web-based entertainment stages and internet business, he constructed areas of strength for a presence that rose above geological limits. Virtual customer facing facades and drawing in satisfied turned out to be amazing assets in overcoming any issues between his business and the worldwide purchaser base.

Be that as it may, the excursion was not without its difficulties. Financial vacillations, administrative obstacles, and social contrasts tried Alex's flexibility. Courageous, he looked for direction from guides who had effectively explored worldwide waters. Their accounts of beating difficulty turned into a wellspring of motivation, bracing Alex's assurance to own his vision.

Alex realized the significance of a diverse and adaptable team as his business grew globally. He encouraged a culture of incorporation, uniting people with shifted foundations and viewpoints. This mixture of gifts ended up being a favorable place for development, permitting the organization to remain on the ball in a steadily developing worldwide market.

One vital crossroads came when Alex protected an organization with an eminent abroad merchant. This essential union extended his market reach as well as opened ways to new open doors for coordinated effort. In the global business landscape, it was evidence of the transformative power of strong partnerships that benefit both parties.

In the midst of the victories and difficulties, Alex stayed focused on manageability. He carried out eco-accommodating practices across his production network, reverberating with earth cognizant customers around the world. This lined up with worldwide patterns as well as situated his image as a dependable player in the global market.

The far reaching influence of Alex's worldwide market systems was felt in meeting rooms as well as in the networks his business contacted. Work creation, ability advancement, and social trade became intrinsic side-effects of his global development. The once-neighborhood endeavor had developed into a worldwide power for positive change.

As Alex thought about his extraordinary excursion, he understood that the way to outcome in the worldwide market lay in essential preparation as well as in embracing change with a receptive outlook. His business had grown, and the tenacity with which he pursued innovation had become a model for others who aspired to go beyond borders.

Alex Turner's story is a reminder of the lasting power of innovation, perseverance, and a visionary spirit in the fabric of global business. His excursion, set apart by difficulties and wins, reverberates as a moving account for those really hoping for growing their organizations past lines.

Overview of Global Market Expansion

Worldwide market development alludes to the course of organizations expanding their tasks past their homegrown boundaries to arrive at global business sectors. This peculiarity has picked up critical speed in many years, driven by globalization, mechanical headways, and expanding interconnectedness. This outline will dive into the key variables impacting worldwide market extension, its advantages and difficulties, and give instances of fruitful procedures.

1. Drivers of Worldwide Market Development:

Globalization: The interconnectedness of economies has advanced rapidly because of progressions in correspondence, transportation, and economic deals. Organizations are constrained to investigate worldwide business sectors to take advantage of assorted buyer bases.

Mechanical Headways: The ascent of the web and advanced innovations has worked with worldwide correspondence and exchanges. Web based business stages, computerized advertising, and online presence assume significant parts in growing business sector reach.

Financial Learning experiences: Companies look for growth opportunities in foreign markets where the economy might be doing better. Developing business sectors frequently present undiscovered customer bases and potential for expanded benefits.

Cutthroat Tensions: Extreme rivalry in homegrown business sectors urges organizations to investigate new regions to keep up with or improve their piece of the pie.

2. Advantages of Worldwide Market Development:

Expanded Income: Getting to new business sectors gives potential open doors to higher deals and income, especially while focusing on districts with developing purchaser interest.

Diversification: Extending universally permits organizations to enhance their client base, diminishing reliance on a solitary market and relieving chances related with monetary variances in unambiguous locales.

Economies of Scale: Bigger market presence empowers organizations to accomplish economies of scale, prompting cost decreases underway, conveyance, and showcasing.

Upgraded Development: Openness to assorted showcases frequently cultivates development, as organizations adjust items and administrations to meet the one of a kind requirements and inclinations of various societies.

3. Difficulties of Worldwide Market Extension:

Social Contrasts: Understanding and adjusting to assorted societies is basic for progress. Confounding social subtleties can prompt correspondence breakdowns and ineffective promoting techniques.

Administrative Consistence: Exploring different administrative conditions can be intricate. Organizations need to comply with various regulations, exchange limitations, and consistency guidelines in every nation of activity.

Calculated Difficulties: Overseeing supply chains, appropriation organizations, and transportation across boundaries can be testing, requiring cautious preparation and coordination.

Cash Vacillations: Swapping scale unpredictability presents monetary dangers for organizations participating in global exchange. Unexpected money changes can affect expenses, evaluating, and benefits.

4. Fruitful Methodologies for Worldwide Market Extension:

Intensive Statistical surveying: Far reaching statistical surveying is fundamental to figure out the main interest group, rivalry, and administrative scene in each new market.

Key Organizations: Working together with nearby accomplices can give significant bits of knowledge, lay out validity, and work with a smoother market section.

Tweaked Showcasing: Fitting advertising techniques to suit the inclinations and social subtleties of each market improves the odds of coming out on top.

Adaptability: Adaptability is urgent despite changing economic situations. Organizations that can adjust their items and procedures to neighborhood inclinations will more often than not flourish.

5. Instances of Worldwide Market Extension:

McDonald's: This cheap food goliath has effectively extended its worldwide impression, adjusting menus to nearby preferences and inclinations. McDonald's epitomizes the significance of limitation in worldwide market procedures.

Samsung: The South Korean hardware monster has decisively entered different business sectors around the world, offering a scope of items fit to nearby necessities while keeping a reliable worldwide brand picture.

Alibaba: The Chinese internet business monster has extended past its homegrown market to turn into a worldwide player. Alibaba's prosperity lies in utilizing innovation and shaping organizations to explore different worldwide business sectors.

All in all, worldwide market development is a complex yet fundamental system for organizations hoping to flourish in the cutting edge monetary scene. While it presents various difficulties, the possible advantages regarding income, expansion, and development make it a convincing road for development. Effective development requires cautious preparation, versatility, and a profound comprehension of the different business sectors where an organization works.

Importance of Going Beyond Borders

Businesses looking for long-term success and sustained growth must expand into global markets. In an interconnected world, going past lines gives a heap of chances, cultivating development, broadening, and expanded market reach. This essential move is urgent for utilizing undiscovered business sectors, relieving chances related with local monetary variances, and remaining cutthroat in the unique business scene.

The diversification of revenue streams is one of the primary benefits of entering international markets. Depending entirely on a homegrown market opens a business to the dangers related with nearby monetary slumps, changes in shopper conduct, and administrative vulnerabilities. Companies can strengthen their financial structures by expanding globally, making them less susceptible to market-specific obstacles. Enhancement likewise permits organizations to benefit from the qualities of various economies, acquiring strength through a fair arrangement of business sectors.

Additionally, expanding your customer base increases your chances of making more money and sales. A worldwide market development procedure empowers organizations to take advantage of new socioeconomics with shifting requirements and inclinations. This expansion of client profiles expands the purchaser base as well as gives significant bits of knowledge to item transformation and advancement. The development of goods and services that satisfy a wide range of preferences and needs is facilitated by an understanding of various markets, thereby enhancing the brand's competitive position.

Besides, going past lines encourages development and multifaceted joint effort. Openness to various business sectors frequently expects organizations to adjust their items or administrations to satisfy neighborhood inclinations and guidelines. This variation cycle animates imagination and development as organizations endeavor to remain pertinent in different conditions. Working together with experts and accomplices from various societies brings new points of view and approaches, cultivating a culture of development inside the association.

Worldwide development likewise permits organizations to exploit cost efficiencies and economies of scale. Fabricating and obtaining in various locales can prompt lower creation costs, better admittance to unrefined components, and further developed store network flexibility. Organizations can improve their tasks by decisively circulating creation and coordinated operations, subsequently expanding productivity and lessening general expenses. This proficiency acquires an upper hand in evaluating, making items more alluring to purchasers in various business sectors.

The significance of going past boundaries stretches out to ability securing and human asset the board. Working in various nations gives admittance to a different pool of ability with fluctuated abilities and viewpoints. This variety improves critical thinking capacities and advances a more comprehensive and versatile hierarchical culture. By providing opportunities for international experience and career advancement, businesses that embrace global expansion tend to attract top-tier talent.

Besides, global development can go about as a gamble moderation system. Depending entirely on a homegrown market opens organizations to the inborn dangers related with that particular locale, like political shakiness, financial slumps, or changes in administrative structures. Companies can lessen the impact of localized risks by expanding operations across multiple countries, resulting in a more resilient and long-lasting business model.

As a result of advancements in technology and communication, the world has transformed into a global marketplace where customers are connected and well-informed. Trends and innovations can quickly spread across borders thanks to this interconnectedness. Organizations that work solely inside their homegrown business sectors might pass up chances to take on or trailblazer new innovations, restricting their seriousness on a worldwide scale. Companies can stay ahead of technological developments by expanding beyond national borders, allowing them to remain adaptable and responsive to shifting customer expectations.

In addition, worldwide development is fundamental for getting to developing business sectors with high development potential. As creating economies keep on developing, they present worthwhile open doors for organizations trying to lay out a traction in undiscovered domains. Organizations that grow universally can gain by the rising working class in developing business sectors, making new business sectors for their items and administrations. This proactive methodology positions organizations to profit from the development directions of these economies, getting an upper hand over those bound to develop markets.

it is impossible to overstate the significance of expanding internationally for global market expansion. The upsides of broadening, expanded market reach, development, cost efficiencies, ability obtaining, risk relief, and admittance to developing business sectors altogether add to the drawn out progress and supportability of organizations. Companies that embrace international expansion are better positioned to overcome obstacles, seize opportunities, and thrive in the dynamic global marketplace in a world where interconnectedness defines the business landscape.

Chapter 1 Market Research and Analysis

Statistical surveying and examination assume essential parts in molding powerful worldwide market techniques for organizations. In a consistently developing and interconnected world, understanding business sector elements is pivotal for organizations looking for supportable development and seriousness. This exhaustive interaction includes social events, deciphering, and applying information to acquire bits of knowledge into buyer conduct, industry patterns, and cutthroat scenes.

I. Significance of Statistical surveying:
Statistical surveying is the establishment whereupon fruitful worldwide market systems are assembled. It assists organizations with distinguishing open doors, evaluating dangers, and pursuing informed choices. Companies can tailor their products or services to meet changing demands by analyzing consumer preferences, purchasing habits, and emerging trends.

II. Kinds of Statistical surveying:

Primary Study:
Leading reviews, meetings, and center gatherings straightforwardly with interest groups.
Getting firsthand data about inclinations, feelings, and ways of behaving.

Auxiliary Exploration:
Dissecting existing information from sources like industry reports, government distributions, and scholarly examinations.
Acquiring experiences into market size, contenders, and macroeconomic variables.

Subjective Exploration:
using methods like in-depth interviews and observations to investigate attitudes, motivations, and perceptions.
Revealing hidden factors that impact customer choices.

Quantitative Exploration:

Utilizing factual strategies to dissect mathematical information accumulated through reviews, tests, or organized interviews.
Getting quantifiable experiences into market patterns, socioeconomics, and purchaser inclinations.

III. Market Investigation:
Market investigation includes deciphering gathered information to observe examples, patterns, and open doors. For developing effective strategies for the global market, this step is essential.

SWOT Evaluation:
Distinguishing Qualities, Shortcomings, Open doors, and Dangers.
Knowledge of both the company's internal capabilities and external influences.

Contender Investigation:
Assessing contenders' assets, shortcomings, piece of the pie, and systems.
Benchmarking against industry pioneers to distinguish regions for development.

Shopper Conduct Investigation:
Concentrating on buying designs, dynamic cycles, and brand dependability.
Adjusting methodologies to line up with buyer inclinations and assumptions.

IV. Worldwide Market Systems:
Outfitted with strong statistical surveying and investigation, organizations can foster successful worldwide market methodologies that expand valuable open doors and relieve gambles.

Globalization as well as localization:
Offsetting worldwide normalization with neighborhood variation.

Perceiving social subtleties, legitimate systems, and purchaser ways of behaving in various business sectors.

Diversification:
Extending item or administration contributions to take care of assorted market portions.

Lessening reliance on unambiguous items or areas to improve versatility.

Organizations and Partnerships:
Teaming up with nearby organizations, providers, or merchants.

Utilizing laid out organizations to explore new business sectors.

Integration of Innovation and Technology:
Embracing arising innovations to upgrade items or administrations.

Remaining in front of industry patterns through persistent advancement.

Risk The executives:
Expecting and tending to likely dangers, including financial variances, international issues, and administrative changes.

Carrying out systems to protect against unexpected difficulties.

V. Contextual analyses:
Analyzing fruitful worldwide market techniques from different enterprises gives important bits of knowledge into compelling methodologies.

Apple Inc.:
Offsetting worldwide marking with limited advertising methodologies.

Adjusting items to meet explicit local inclinations while keeping a steady brand picture.

Procter and Bet:
Utilizing broad statistical surveying to comprehend assorted shopper needs.

Creating items custom-made to nearby inclinations while keeping a worldwide brand presence.

Toyota:
Embracing a cross breed approach by offering both worldwide and locale explicit models.
Ceaselessly adjusting items in view of market criticism and mechanical headways.

VI. Arising Patterns:
Keeping up to date with arising patterns is critical for supported progress in worldwide business sectors.

Sustainability:
Tending to natural worries and embracing eco-accommodating practices.
satisfying consumer demands for sustainable and ethically produced goods.

Digital Revolution:
utilizing digital platforms for customer engagement, sales, and marketing.
Bridling information examination for continuous bits of knowledge and customized encounters.

Online business Extension:
Gaining by the developing pattern of internet shopping.
Creating consistent and secure web-based stages to arrive at a worldwide client base.

Successful global market strategies are fundamentally based on market research and analysis. It is easier for businesses to navigate the complexities of the global market when they make investments in comprehending consumer behavior, industry trends, and competitive landscapes. Companies can develop strategies that not only address current challenges but also anticipate and capitalize on emerging opportunities, ensuring long-term growth and sustainability, by embracing innovation, collaboration, and adaptability.

Conducting Global Market Research

Directing worldwide statistical surveying is a critical stage for organizations trying to extend their range and flourish in an undeniably interconnected world. This complete cycle includes assembling and dissecting data about target markets, purchasers, contenders, and industry patterns on a worldwide scale. Effective worldwide statistical surveying gives important experiences as well as helps in settling on informed choices, moderating dangers, and distinguishing potential open doors for development. In this article, we'll investigate the critical stages and contemplations associated with leading compelling worldwide statistical surveying.

Understanding the Value of Conducting Research on Global Markets Expanding into international markets carries significant growth potential but also a number of unique challenges. Worldwide statistical surveying fills in as the establishment for conquering these difficulties by giving a profound comprehension of different business sectors, purchaser ways of behaving, and administrative conditions. It assists organizations with fitting their methodologies to meet the particular necessities and inclinations of various districts, accordingly improving the probability of accomplishment.

Key Stages in Directing Worldwide Statistical surveying

Characterize Targets and Extension:
The first step is to clearly define the goals of your global market research. What are you hoping to accomplish? Whether it's entering another market, figuring out purchaser inclinations, or assessing contests, laying out clear objectives will direct your examination endeavors. To keep your research focused and pertinent, define its scope.

Recognize Target Markets:
Distinguish the particular nations or locales you mean to target. Consider factors, for example, market size, development potential, social subtleties, and administrative conditions. Focus on business sectors in view of their arrangement with your business objectives and assets.

Assemble Optional Information:
Begin by gathering optional information from existing sources, for example, market reports, government distributions, and industry investigations. This underlying step assists in grasping the general market with finishing, central members, and existing patterns. It additionally helps with recognizing holes in information that might require essential examination.

Direct Essential Exploration:
Essential examination includes gathering firsthand data straightforwardly from the interest group. This can be accomplished through reviews, interviews, center gatherings, and perceptions. Tailor your

examination techniques to suit social inclinations and language subtleties in each market.

Think about Social Contrasts:
Social varieties essentially influence buyer ways of behaving and inclinations. Recognize and regard these distinctions while planning overviews or directing meetings. Guarantee that your exploration instruments are socially delicate to get exact and significant reactions.

Contender Examination:
Break down the cutthroat scene in each target market. Recognize key contenders, their assets, shortcomings, and market situating. Understanding contender techniques gives significant bits of knowledge to fostering an upper hand.

Assess the Regulatory Setting:
Various districts have particular administrative systems that can influence business tasks. Research and comprehend the legitimate and administrative prerequisites in each market to guarantee consistency and limit chances.

Use Innovation and Information Examination:
To speed up the research process, make use of cutting-edge technologies and data analytics tools. Robotization and information driven bits of knowledge upgrade the exactness and proficiency of worldwide statistical surveying, empowering quicker independent direction.

Survey Monetary Elements:
Assess financial factors, for example, Gross domestic product, expansion rates, and money solidness.

Understanding the monetary environment in target markets assists in anticipating with promoting potential and surveying the monetary reasonability of extension.

Validation and feedback from customers:

Accumulate criticism from likely clients through experimental runs projects or item models. This immediate cooperation gives ongoing experiences and approves the market interest for your item or administration.

Obstacles and Options Language Barriers:

Language contrasts can present difficulties in correspondence and information translation. Guarantee that overviews and exploration materials are precisely meant to catch the expected importance.

Privacy and security of data:

Various locales might have differing information assurance guidelines. To build consumer trust and avoid legal issues, prioritize data security and privacy compliance.

Adaptability:

Markets develop, and shopper inclinations change over the long haul. Incorporate adaptability into your examination way to deal with adjusting to dynamic economic situations and arising patterns.

Neighborhood Associations:

Laying out nearby organizations can work with a smoother market section. Work together with neighborhood organizations or specialists who comprehend the social subtleties and business scene.

Leading worldwide statistical surveying is a complex yet imperative cycle for organizations trying to flourish with the worldwide stage. It requires an essential methodology, social responsiveness, and a guarantee to get-together exact and pertinent information. Effective worldwide statistical surveying enables organizations to pursue informed choices, limit gambles, and exploit valuable open doors, at last making ready for supportable global development.

Analyzing Target Markets and Competitors

Investigating objective business sectors and contenders is a critical part of any business methodology. This cycle includes assessing the qualities of likely clients and understanding the scene wherein an organization works. By directing an exhaustive examination, organizations can settle on informed choices, tailor their promoting endeavors, and gain an upper hand on the lookout.

Understanding Objective Business sectors:

Distinguishing and understanding objective business sectors is the groundwork of an effective business system. An objective market is a particular gathering of customers that an organization intends to reach with its items or administrations. Businesses must take into account a variety of factors in order to effectively analyze target markets.

Demographics: Begin by looking at segment factors like age, orientation, pay, training, and occupation. Understanding these elements assists in making items and advertising messages that reverberate with the target group.

Psychographics: Jump further into the psychographics of the objective market by breaking down their way of life, values, interests, and ways of behaving. This data permits organizations to interface with shoppers on a more private level, upgrading the viability of promoting efforts.

Geographic Area: Consider the geographic area of the objective market. Various locales might have novel inclinations, social subtleties, and financial circumstances that impact purchaser conduct.

Aspects of behavior: Assess customer conduct, including buying designs, brand faithfulness, and dynamic cycles. Businesses can use this information to adapt their offerings and marketing strategies to customers' preferences.

Necessities and Inclinations: Distinguish the necessities, inclinations, and problem areas of the objective market. By tending to these angles, organizations can foster items that truly fulfill purchaser needs and hang out in the cutthroat scene.

Contender Examination: Understanding contenders is essentially as critical as realizing the objective market. Contender examination includes surveying the qualities and shortcomings of opponent organizations to recognize valuable open doors and dangers on the lookout.

Recognize Competitors: Begin by distinguishing immediate and roundabout contenders. Direct contenders offer comparable items or administrations, while circuitous contenders might give choices that satisfy similar requirements.

SWOT Examination: Direct a thorough SWOT examination for every contender. Assess their assets, shortcomings, open doors, and dangers. This examination helps in understanding the cutthroat scene and distinguishing regions where a business can beat rivals.

Portion of the overall industry: Determine each competitor's market share to evaluate their relative position in the industry. Businesses are able to identify potential areas of growth when they are aware of the market share, which provides insights into the intensity of the competition.

Item and Evaluating Methodology: Break down the items and valuing procedures of contenders. A company's product development and pricing decisions can be influenced by its knowledge of successful products and their pricing.

Showcasing and Marking: Analyze the promoting and marking techniques of contenders. Distinguish key messages, channels, and strategies utilized by opponents to draw in with the main interest group. This data can direct the improvement of a separated and powerful promoting methodology.

Integration of Competitor and Target Market Analysis:

Integrating these insights into a comprehensive business strategy is crucial after independent analyses of target markets and competitors.

Recognize Remarkable Selling Suggestion (USP): Utilize the comprehension of target markets and contender examination to recognize a Remarkable Selling Recommendation. A USP separates a business from contenders and requests to the particular requirements and inclinations of the objective market.

Market Division: Section the objective market in view of the examination. This permits organizations to fit their promoting endeavors to various sections, guaranteeing a more customized and compelling methodology.

Opportunity ID: Recognize valuable open doors in the market by surveying holes or neglected needs that contenders may not be tending to. This can prompt the improvement of imaginative items or administrations that take care of explicit client requests.

Mitigation of Risk: Perceive expected dangers and difficulties presented by contenders. Understanding their techniques and market situating empowers organizations to proactively address dangers and relieve gambles.

Any business's success depends on continuously and dynamically analyzing its target markets and competitors. Businesses can use it to align their products, marketing efforts, and overall approach with the ever-changing requirements of their target audience and the landscape of competition by providing a foundation for strategic decision-making. Ordinary reassessment and variation of these examinations are critical to remaining ahead in a cutthroat market climate.

Chapter 2
Legal and Regulatory Considerations

Businesses' global market strategies are shaped and guided by legal and regulatory considerations. Exploring the perplexing scene of worldwide trade requires a thorough comprehension of the regulations and guidelines that oversee different wards. This article investigates key parts of legitimate and administrative contemplations with regards to worldwide market procedures, looking at the difficulties and potential open doors they present for organizations working on a worldwide scale.

1. Worldwide Exchange Regulations:
Compliance with international trade laws is an essential legal consideration for global market strategies. Associations should comply with arrangements like the World Exchange Association (WTO) rules and local exchange settlements. Levies, exchange boundaries, and

product/import guidelines fluctuate across nations, affecting the development of labor and products. A viable worldwide market methodology expects organizations to keep up to date with advancing exchange approaches to limit chances and gain by arising open doors.

2. Licensed innovation Assurance:
Safeguarding protected innovation (IP) is basic for organizations growing worldwide. Changed legitimate systems with respect to licenses, brand names, and copyrights require a careful comprehension of every locale's regulations. Organizations should carry out powerful systems to defend their IP resources, including enrolling licenses and brand names in applicable nations and creating arrangements that moderate the gamble of encroachment.

3. Conformity to Law:
Worldwide organizations should explore assorted administrative systems in various nations. It is essential to adhere to industry-specific regulations, local laws, and standards. Administrative bodies, for example, the Protections and Trade Commission (SEC) or the European Protections and Markets Authority (ESMA), force explicit prerequisites on monetary divulgences and revealing. Complying with these guidelines guarantees lawful consistency as well as constructs entrusted with partners.

4. Information Insurance and Protection:
The ascent of digitalization has elevated worries about information assurance and security. The General Data Protection Regulation (GDPR) in the

European Union imposes stringent data protection regulations on businesses. A worldwide market system requires a vigorous way to deal with taking care of individual information, enveloping assent components, secure capacity, and the capacity to answer information breaks really.

5. Laws Against Corruption:

The United States Foreign Corrupt Practices Act (FCPA) and the United Kingdom Bribery Act are two examples of anti-corruption laws that have been enacted in many nations. Corruption prevention is a global priority. Adherence to these regulations is crucial for organizations taking part in global business. Executing solid enemy of defilement approaches, leading expected level of effort on colleagues, and giving extensive preparation to workers are critical parts of a consistent worldwide market system.

6. Business Regulations and Work Practices:

Various work regulations and work rehearses across nations require cautious thought while extending a business worldwide. Issues like working hours, wages, and worker freedoms shift generally. In order to foster a positive corporate image and ensure fair and ethical employment practices, a global market strategy must incorporate a thorough understanding of local labor laws.

7. Regulations for the Environment and Sustainability:

With expanding worldwide consciousness of natural issues, organizations are confronting elevated examination in regards to their ecological effect. Complying with manageability guidelines and corporate social obligation (CSR) rehearses is fundamental. Organizations should adjust their worldwide market procedures to ecological guidelines to relieve chances related with resistance and appeal to earth cognizant customers.

8. Political Soundness and Hazard:
Political soundness in a nation straightforwardly impacts the simplicity of carrying on with work. Organizations should evaluate the political scene of target markets, taking into account factors like international strains, government dependability, and the general business-accommodating climate. Integrating political gamble appraisals into worldwide market systems assists organizations with expecting possible difficulties and adjusting their methodologies in a similar manner.

9. Question Goal Systems:
In the global business field, questions might emerge, requiring viable goal components. Grasping the lawful structures for debate goals, like global discretion or intervention, is essential. Remembering question goal provisos for agreements and arrangements gives organizations a reasonable guide for tending to clashes in a fair and proficient way.

10. Social and Moral Contemplations:
Global market strategies ought to take cultural and ethical considerations into account in addition to legal and regulatory aspects. Building positive relationships with stakeholders requires an understanding of local customs,

traditions, and business practices. Adjusting showcasing systems and correspondence styles to line up with social responsive qualities improves an organization's standing and cultivates fruitful worldwide tasks.

Taking everything into account, legitimate and administrative contemplations are fundamental parts of creating and executing viable worldwide market techniques. Organizations should put time and assets in figuring out the complexities of worldwide regulations, economic accords, and administrative scenes to effectively explore the intricacies of the worldwide commercial center. By coordinating legitimate consistency into key preparation, organizations can alleviate chances, assemble entrust with partners, and position themselves for economic development in an undeniably interconnected world.

Understanding International Business Laws

The interactions and transactions between entities in various nations are governed by international business laws, which play an important role in the globalized economy. These regulations envelop a large number of legitimate systems that address different parts of global exchange, speculation, and business tasks. To explore the intricacies of leading business on a worldwide scale, it is fundamental for business visionaries, companies, and legitimate experts to have an exhaustive comprehension of global business regulations.

One critical part of worldwide business regulations is the guideline of cross-line exchange. The rules and principles for the exchange of goods and services between nations are established by international trade law, which is governed by agreements like the WTO treaties. These arrangements plan to advance fair rivalry, dispense with exchange obstructions, and establish an anticipated climate for organizations. Figuring out the standards of streamlined commerce, duties, and non-levy boundaries is fundamental for organizations that took part in global exchange.

One more basic region inside worldwide business regulations is speculation regulation. Reciprocal speculation settlements (Pieces) and multilateral venture arrangements give a legitimate system to safeguard unfamiliar ventures and guarantee a fair and even handed treatment for financial backers. Financial backers should know about the question goal components framed in these arrangements, like mediation, to address clashes that might emerge between the financial backer and the host country.

International business also relies heavily on intellectual property rights. Organizations working worldwide should be knowledgeable in global settlements like the Settlement on Exchange Related Parts of Licensed innovation Privileges (Outings). Safeguarding brand names, licenses, and copyrights is vital for protecting developments and manifestations across borders. To avoid legal disputes and issues related to infringement, it is essential to be aware of the various intellectual property laws in different countries.

Business and work regulations change generally across nations, and global companies should agree with the neighborhood guidelines of every ward where they work. Understanding the distinctions in business contracts, working circumstances, and work norms is basic to guarantee lawful consistency and cultivate positive relations with representatives around the world. Organizations ought to be all around informed about worldwide work associations and shows that address issues like separation, constrained work, and youngster work.

Contract regulation is one more major part of worldwide business. While going into concurrences with parties from various nations, organizations should consider the appropriateness of worldwide shows like the Unified Countries Show on Agreements for the Global Offer of Products (CISG). Experience with the standards of agreement arrangement, execution, and debate goal is fundamental to relieve chances and guarantee enforceability in cross-line exchanges.

The lawful scene for global business is ceaselessly advancing, affected by international turns of events, mechanical progressions, and changes in monetary approaches. For businesses to adapt their strategies and remain compliant, it is essential to remain informed about the most recent developments in international law. Companies are able to make informed decisions and reduce the potential legal risks associated with their international operations by receiving regular updates on trade agreements, sanctions, and legal precedents.

One huge test in worldwide business is exploring the intricacies of assessment regulations. To ensure proper compliance and avoid double taxation, businesses conducting cross-border transactions must be aware of the tax regulations in each jurisdiction. Planning international taxes and comprehending transfer pricing regulations are essential for maximizing operational efficiency and maximizing tax structures.

Consistency against debasement regulations is one more basic part of worldwide business. To prevent bribery and corruption in international transactions, the United States' Foreign Corrupt Practices Act (FCPA) and the United Kingdom's Bribery Act impose stringent regulations on businesses. To reduce legal risks and uphold ethical business practices, it is essential to implement robust anti-corruption compliance programs and conduct due diligence on business partners.

Natural and maintainability regulations have acquired conspicuousness in worldwide business because of developing worries about environmental change and corporate obligation. Organizations working around the world should know about global natural arrangements and nearby guidelines resolving issues like contamination, squandering the executives, and supportable practices. Incorporating naturally mindful practices into business tasks guarantees consistency as well as improves the organization's standing and appeal to ecologically cognizant shoppers.

understanding worldwide business regulations is fundamental for elements working in the worldwide field. From exchange and venture to licensed innovation, work, contracts, charge, hostility to debasement, and ecological guidelines, organizations should explore a complex legitimate scene. Remaining informed, looking for legitimate guidance, and taking on proactive consistent measures are fundamental methodologies to flourish in the dynamic and interconnected universe of global business.

With a strong handle of worldwide business regulations, associations can moderate lawful dangers, cultivate positive associations with partners, and add to a more maintainable and moral worldwide business climate.

Navigating Trade Regulations and Compliance

A crucial aspect of global market strategies is complying with trade regulations. Businesses must adhere to a complex web of international trade laws in an interconnected world to ensure smooth operations and avoid legal pitfalls. This article dives into the vital contemplations for organizations while figuring out procedures to explore exchange guidelines and consistency on the worldwide stage.

Grasping Exchange Guidelines: Exchange guidelines are the standards and approaches laid out by states to administer the progression of labor and products across borders. These guidelines intend to safeguard homegrown businesses, guarantee fair contest, and address public safety concerns. A comprehensive comprehension of the legal frameworks in each country where a business operates or plans to expand is necessary for navigating these regulations.

Due Study and Investigation: Intensive examination and an expected level of investment are pivotal parts of any fruitful worldwide market technique. Target markets' trade regulations, such as tariff rates, import/export restrictions, and documentation requirements, must be well understood by businesses. Directing business sector explicit exploration distinguishes possible difficulties and open doors, empowering organizations to in like manner tailor their methodologies.

Customs Consistence: Customs consistency is a foundation of worldwide exchange. Organizations should guarantee that their merchandise conform to the traditions guidelines of the nations in question. This incorporates exact grouping of items, appropriate valuation, and adherence to naming and bundling necessities. Resistance can bring about postponements, fines, or even capture of merchandise.

Fit Framework (HS) Codes: The Fit Framework (HS) gives a normalized order framework to items exchanged globally. Doling out the right HS code to an item is significant for customs freedom and consistency. Misclassifying items can prompt traditions errors and legitimate outcomes. To accurately classify products under the HS system, businesses should devote time and resources to staff training or technology use.

Economic accords: Understanding territorial and two-sided economic deals is fundamental for advancing worldwide market methodologies. These arrangements can offer particular treatment, like decreased levies or smoothed out customs methods, for organizations working inside and taking an interest in nations. Businesses are able to take advantage of new opportunities and reduce risks by staying informed about changes in trade agreements.

Risk The board: Risk of the executives is basic to exploring exchange guidelines effectively. Organizations ought to distinguish possible dangers, remembering changes for exchange arrangements, international pressures, and financial shakiness. Creating emergency courses of action and expanding supply chains can assist with alleviating the effect of unexpected occasions.

Consistence with Authorizations: When it comes to adhering to international sanctions imposed by governments or regulatory bodies, businesses must exercise extreme caution. Sanctions are frequently executed for political, financial, or security reasons and can limit exchange with explicit nations or substances. A company's reputation could be harmed, severe penalties could be imposed, and legal action could follow if sanctions are ignored or broken.

Record-keeping and documentation: Precise and far reaching documentation is critical for exchange consistency. Organizations ought to keep up with nitty gritty records of exchanges, including solicitations, delivering archives, and authentications of beginning. These records work with customs freedom as well as act as proof of consistency if there should arise an occurrence of reviews or questions.

Innovation Arrangements: In the computerized age, utilizing innovation is principal for proficient exchange consistency. Mechanized frameworks can help with overseeing documentation, observing administrative changes, and guaranteeing exact item order. Carrying out innovation arrangements can smooth out processes, lessen human mistake, and upgrade by and large consistency endeavors.

Worker Preparing: Thoroughly prepared staff is a priceless resource in guaranteeing exchange consistency. Giving continuous preparation on important exchange guidelines, industry best practices, and the successful utilization of innovation enables representatives to explore the intricacies of worldwide exchange. This interest in expertise improvement adds to a culture of consistency inside the association.

Drawing in with Administrative Specialists:

Laying out open lines of correspondence with administrative experts in target markets can be helpful. Ordinary discourse can give experiences into impending administrative changes, explain vulnerabilities, and cultivate positive connections. Drawing in proactively with specialists shows a guarantee to consistency and can prompt smoother collaborations during reviews or examinations.

Exploring exchange guidelines and consistency is a multi-layered challenge for organizations seeking after worldwide market techniques. A proactive methodology, grounded in exhaustive exploration, risk the board, and mechanical joining, is fundamental. Adjusting to developing exchange scenes, remaining informed about administrative changes, and cultivating a culture of consistency are key components in making long haul progress in the worldwide commercial center. Organizations that focus on these viewpoints position themselves to explore the many-sided snare of global exchange guidelines successfully and profit by the valuable open doors introduced by an interconnected world.

Chapter 3
Cultural and Linguistic Challenges

Exploring worldwide market systems includes tending to different social and semantic difficulties that can fundamentally influence the progress of organizations. As organizations extend their activities across borders, they should be receptive to the assorted social settings and semantic subtleties inborn in various locales. The significance of comprehending linguistic and cultural obstacles to the creation and implementation of global market strategies is the subject of this essay.

Cultural Obstacles:
Variety in Values and Standards:
Social variety is a sign of the worldwide commercial center, and each culture brings its own arrangement of values and standards. Organizations should be aware of these varieties to keep away from social errors that could endanger business connections.

Methods of communication:
Successful correspondence is vital in worldwide business. Various societies might have particular correspondence styles, going from immediate and unequivocal to backhanded and implied. Understanding these subtleties is

fundamental for fruitful talks, promoting, and in general business collaborations.

Moral Contrasts:

Moral norms change around the world, and what might be viewed as adequate in one culture may be seen as unscrupulous in another. In order to maintain their reputation and adhere to international business standards, businesses must navigate these differences ethically.

Hierarchy and Making Decisions:

The various leveled construction and dynamic cycles can fluctuate broadly among societies. A few societies might esteem a more varied leveled approach, while others favor a cooperative dynamic cycle. To meet the requirements of the local market, businesses must modify their management styles.

Social Awareness in Showcasing:

To appeal to a wide range of customers, marketing strategies need to take into account cultural differences. The cultural connotations of colors, symbols, and even product positioning can vary. An oversight in such a manner can prompt promoting efforts that are insufficient or, more regrettable, hostile.

Problems with the Language:

Language Obstructions:

Language contrasts represent a critical obstacle in worldwide business. Miscommunications can happen at different levels - from item data and promoting content to discussions. Putting resources into proficient interpretation administrations is pivotal to guarantee precise correspondence.

Informal Articulations and Humor:

Informal articulations and go along with can be trying to precisely interpret. What may be a smart promoting trademark in one language could lose its expected importance or even be misjudged in another. Organizations should be aware of these phonetic nuances.

Lawful and Administrative Consistence:
Understanding the neighborhood language is vital for consistency with legitimate and administrative necessities. Authoritative archives, agreements, and agreements should be precisely meant to stay away from any misconceptions that could prompt lawful issues.

Specialized Language and Industry-Explicit Phrasing:
Enterprises frequently have their own arrangement of specialized language and wording. Deciphering these terms precisely is critical, particularly in areas like innovation, medication, or regulation, where accuracy is essential.

Management of a Multilingual Workforce:
Dealing with a multilingual labor force requires compelling correspondence methodologies. Language contrasts can prompt mistaken assumptions among workers, affecting joint effort and efficiency. Giving language preparation and establishing a multilingual-accommodating workplace is fundamental.

Techniques to Beat Difficulties:
Social Insight Preparing:
Giving social insight to workers helps them comprehend and explore social contrasts. This preparation ought to cover correspondence styles, discussion

strategies, and social subtleties well defined for the districts where the organization works.

Nearby Associations:
Working with partners in the local community can provide valuable insights into the linguistic and cultural landscape. Nearby accomplices bring a comprehension of market subtleties, shopper conduct, and compelling correspondence procedures inside their district.

Tweaked Promoting Techniques:
Fitting promoting procedures to each social setting is critical. This includes adjusting publicizing materials, item situating, and limited time exercises to line up with the qualities and inclinations of the ideal interest group in a particular locale.

Interest in Language Administrations:
Organizations ought to put resources into proficient language administrations, including interpretation, understanding, and limitation. Using native speakers and linguists helps avoid costly blunders and ensures accurate communication.

Adaptability and Versatility:
An adaptable and versatile methodology is vital to conquering social and phonetic difficulties. Organizations should be available to change their methodologies in view of criticism and encounters in various business sectors, considering ceaseless improvement.

businesses must approach international expansion with a nuanced understanding of diverse cultures and languages because the global market presents cultural and linguistic challenges. By tending to these difficulties decisively, organizations can have areas of strength for fabricating market procedures that reverberate with nearby crowds, encourage positive connections, and eventually drive progress in the mind boggling and interconnected universe of worldwide business.

Adapting to Cultural Differences

Adjusting to social contrasts is foremost in creating compelling worldwide market techniques. In an interconnected world, organizations work across assorted societies, each with its exceptional standards, values, and ways of behaving. Neglecting to comprehend and adjust to these social subtleties can bring about miscommunication, misconceptions, and eventually, the disappointment of worldwide market drives.

One vital part of adjusting to social contrasts is language. Language obstructions can block viable correspondence and upset the effective execution of worldwide market procedures. To address this, organizations should put resources into interpretation administrations, restriction, and socially delicate correspondence materials. Past strict interpretation, it's significant to think about sayings, social references, and subtleties to precisely pass on messages. Furthermore, employing nearby staff who are capable in the language and comprehend the social setting can upgrade correspondence and fabricate entrust with neighborhood markets.

Social varieties in customer conduct are another basic element. Inclinations, buying propensities, and dynamic cycles vary across societies. An effective worldwide market technique requires a profound comprehension of these varieties. Directing careful statistical surveying and customer concentrates on in each target district is fundamental. This knowledge can help with product modifications, pricing plans, and marketing strategies that are tailored to each market's unique cultural preferences.

Normal practices and values likewise assume a critical part in adjusting worldwide market methodologies. What might be OK in one culture could be considered improper in another. For example, promoting that stresses independence might reverberate well in Western societies however may not be generally welcomed in collectivist social orders. Organizations need to adjust their showcasing messages with the common accepted practices to keep away from social cold-heartedness and backfire.

Legitimate and administrative contrasts across nations add one more layer of intricacy. A fruitful worldwide market methodology requires consistence with nearby regulations and guidelines. This includes grasping the express guidelines as well as the social and moral contemplations that might influence business activities. Exploring this scene requires a vigorous legitimate group and organizations with neighborhood specialists who can give experiences into the lawful and administrative structures of each market.

One of the most important aspects of adapting to cultural differences is developing strong relationships with stakeholders in the local community. This incorporates manufacturing associations with nearby organizations, teaming up with government offices, and drawing in with neighborhood networks. Fostering these connections requires a veritable interest in and regard for the nearby culture. Taking part in corporate social obligation drives that line up with the upsides of the local area can assist with building a positive standing and cultivate generosity.

When adapting global market strategies to cultural differences, adaptability is essential. Approaches that prevail in one market may not be guaranteed to work in another. Businesses need to be willing to adjust their strategies in response to feedback and shifting cultural dynamics. This requires nonstop checking of market patterns, shopper ways of behaving, and social movements. Being willing to adapt strategies and learn from mistakes is another component of flexibility.

Employees can help ensure that teams understand and appreciate cultural differences by participating in cross-cultural training. This preparation can cover correspondence styles, business behavior, and social awareness. By furnishing representatives with the information and abilities to explore different social conditions, organizations can improve cooperation, lessen errors, and encourage a more comprehensive and viable worldwide labor force.

Innovation can be utilized to connect social holes in worldwide market methodologies. Virtual coordinated effort apparatuses, increased reality, and man-made brainpower can work with correspondence and figuring out across various societies. Businesses can use these technologies to gather real-time data on cultural trends and consumer behavior for market analysis.

global market strategies cannot succeed without adapting to cultural differences. From language and customer conduct to normal practices and lawful contemplations, organizations should explore an intricate snare of social subtleties. Embracing variety, putting resources into social skill, and staying adaptable are fundamental components of a fruitful worldwide market approach. Thus, organizations can extend their scope as well as fabricate reasonable and significant associations with customers and partners around the world.

Overcoming Language Barriers in Global Business

In global business, it is essential to overcome language barriers for effective communication, relationship building, and collaboration success. In an undeniably interconnected world, where organizations work on a worldwide scale, phonetic variety can present difficulties. In any case, with key methodologies and mechanical progressions, associations can explore these hindrances and make a more comprehensive and effective business climate.

First and foremost, putting resources into language variety inside the association is fundamental. Employees' personal skills will improve as a result of being encouraged to learn and be proficient in multiple languages, which will also make the workforce more adaptable. This can be accomplished through language preparing programs, language trade drives, and social awareness studios. By cultivating a multilingual climate, organizations can engage their representatives to discuss really with worldwide accomplices, clients, and partners.

In addition, embracing innovation is significant in beating language hindrances. Interpretation apparatuses and programming have developed fundamentally, offering constant language interpretation that works with smooth correspondence. These devices, for example, machine interpretation and language handling applications, assist with overcoming any issues between people who communicate in various dialects. Incorporating these advances into everyday business tasks can smooth out correspondence processes and limit misconceptions.

Furthermore, using proficient mediators and interpreters when essential can fundamentally improve correspondence exactness. In circumstances where exact comprehension is essential, like exchanges, agreements, or high-stakes gatherings, having a talented translator can forestall misinterpretations and guarantee that all gatherings included are in total agreement. Whether they are powered by AI or humans, translation services improve the clarity and efficiency of global business communication.

Social mindfulness is one more key part of beating language hindrances. Understanding the subtleties of different societies can forestall miscommunication and cultivate positive connections. Organizations ought to put resources into multifaceted preparation for representatives, accentuating the significance of social awareness in correspondence. Monitoring social standards, decorum, and correspondence styles can assist with exploring possible traps and reinforce global business connections.

Besides, advancing clear and brief correspondence is fundamental in defeating language obstructions. Utilizing plain language, keeping away from complex language, and working on messages can upgrade understanding across language contrasts. This training is especially significant in composed correspondence, where mistaken assumptions can without much of a stretch emerge because of language subtleties. By focusing on lucidity, organizations can diminish the gamble of confusion and advance successful multifaceted correspondence.

Worldwide organizations ought to likewise consider laying out a most widely used language inside their association, a typical language that fills in as an extension between workers of various etymological foundations. This can be English by and large, given its broad use as a global business language. By empowering workers to impart in a typical language, organizations can smooth out inner cycles and guarantee a predictable way to deal with culturally diverse cooperation.

Notwithstanding semantic contemplations, making comprehensive correspondence channels is crucial. Giving composed materials, introductions, and other specialized devices in various dialects can take care of the different etymological requirements of partners. This comprehensive methodology exhibits a guarantee to obliging different semantic foundations, causing all gatherings to feel esteemed and comprehended.

Cooperation stages and undertaking the board instruments that help multilingual points of interaction additionally add to defeating language obstructions. These devices empower groups to work flawlessly across borders, sharing data and updates in a way that is open to everybody, no matter what their local language. The significance of inclusivity in global business practices is reaffirmed by the acceptance of technology that makes it easier to collaborate in multiple languages.

Customary criticism systems are vital for surveying the viability of correspondence techniques in a multicultural and multilingual business climate. Empowering open correspondence channels where workers can communicate concerns or propose upgrades encourages a culture of persistent improvement. By effectively looking for criticism, organizations can adjust their correspondence techniques to address explicit difficulties and improve general viability in beating language hindrances.

conquering language boundaries in worldwide business requires an all encompassing methodology that consolidates language variety inside the association, mechanical arrangements, social mindfulness, and clear correspondence rehearses. Businesses can create an inclusive and productive environment that encourages international collaboration that is successful by investing in these strategies. Embracing semantic variety upgrades correspondence as well as positions associations to flourish in the interconnected and socially rich worldwide business scene.

Chapter 4 Market Entry Strategies

Market section systems assume a significant part in the outcome of organizations looking to venture into the worldwide market. The development of an efficient strategy for the global market takes on greater significance as businesses strive to enter new markets and take advantage of global opportunities. This article will dive into different market passage methodologies, investigating their subtleties and contemplations for organizations exploring the powerful scene of worldwide business.

Understanding the Strategy of Global Markets:

Entering the worldwide market requires an extensive and thoroughly examined system that lines up with the organization's objectives, assets, and the complexities of the objective market. The procedure ought to envelop an intensive investigation of economic situations, social subtleties, legitimate systems, and rivalry.

1. Exporting:

Sending out remains as one of the most direct passage systems, including the offer of items or administrations to unfamiliar business sectors. Businesses with limited resources or those testing the waters before making a larger investment would benefit most from this strategy. Direct exporting, in which a company manages its own distribution, or indirect exporting through agents or distributors are two options.

2. Franchising and licensing:

Permitting and diversifying offer a less capital-escalated strategy for worldwide development. In exchange for fees or royalties, intellectual property rights, such as patents, trademarks, or technology, are granted to a foreign entity through licensing. This idea is extended to business models through franchising, which enables foreign businesses to replicate the established brand and business model.

3. Joint Endeavors and Key Collisions:

Going into joint endeavors or shaping key coalitions with neighborhood accomplices can be an essential move to explore new business sectors. Working together with nearby organizations gives experiences into social subtleties, administrative conditions, and customer conduct. It likewise shares the dangers and expenses of market passage, making it an alluring choice for organizations looking for a reasonable methodology.

4. Unfamiliar Direct Speculation (FDI):

Unfamiliar Direct Speculation includes laying out an actual presence in an unfamiliar market, commonly through auxiliaries, branches, or completely claimed elements. This methodology considers more noteworthy command over activities however requires critical monetary responsibility and a top to bottom comprehension of nearby economic situations. FDI is normal in businesses like assembling, where vicinity to the market is vital.

5. Online business and Computerized Stages:

The global market landscape has changed as a result of the rise of digital platforms and e-commerce. Utilizing on the web channels empowers organizations to arrive at global clients without laying out an actual presence. Companies that deal in digital goods, software, or services stand to gain the most from this strategy.

Strategies for Entering the Global Market:

The selection of a market entry strategy is influenced by a number of factors, which businesses must carefully consider to ensure success:

Market Qualities:

Breaking down the objective market's size, development potential, and cutthroat scene is pivotal.

Grasping social inclinations, customer conduct, and market patterns helps with fitting items and methodologies.

Administrative Climate:

Consistence with nearby regulations and guidelines is fundamental to stay away from legitimate difficulties.

Figuring out exchange hindrances, levies, and import/trade guidelines is critical for consistent activities.

Risk Resistance:

Surveying the organization's gamble resistance decides the degree of buy-in and obligation to a specific market.

Political, financial, and money dangers ought to be painstakingly assessed.

Asset Accessibility:

The accessibility of monetary, human, and mechanical assets impacts the achievability of specific section methodologies.

Organizations should adjust their abilities to the requests of the picked technique.

Situation of competition:

Dissecting existing contenders and potential contestants assists in creating techniques that give an upper hand.

Separation and development become basic components in a jam-packed market.

Difficulties and Alleviation Techniques:

Worldwide market section isn't without difficulties, and organizations should explore intricacies to guarantee economical achievement.

Social Responsiveness:
Building rapport with customers is made easier by adapting products and marketing strategies to local cultures.

Utilizing nearby staff or advisors acquainted with social subtleties is valuable.

Stability in the economy and politics:
Risks from political and economic instability can be mitigated by diversifying operations across stable markets.

Keeping up to date with international improvements helps in proactive gamification of the executives.

Legitimate Consistence:
Working together with lawful specialists and nearby guides guarantees consistency with unpredictable administrative systems.

Routinely refreshing lawful information to adjust to changing guidelines is significant.

Innovation Coordination:
Incorporating innovation across borders requires cautious preparation and thought of framework contrasts.

Executing versatile and versatile innovations upholds consistent worldwide activities.

Production network The executives:
Creating strong inventory network networks limits strategic difficulties and guarantees opportune item conveyance.
Laying out elective providers and appropriation channels adds versatility to the inventory network.

Contextual analyses:
The successful market entry strategies of well-known businesses can provide useful insights.

McDonald's:
McDonald's worldwide achievement comes from adjusting its menu to neighborhood tastes, social inclinations, and strict contemplations.
Vital associations with neighborhood providers and franchisees add to the brand's worldwide presence.

Tesla:
Tesla's worldwide extension includes a blend of trading, unfamiliar direct venture, and vital organizations.
The organization tailors its showcasing systems to line up with the exceptional attributes of each market.

Creating a compelling worldwide market methodology requires a nuanced comprehension of market elements, social complexities, and the serious scene. Organizations should carefully assess section choices, taking into account factors like market qualities, administrative conditions, and asset accessibility. The likelihood of success is increased by overcoming obstacles through cultural adaptation, legal compliance, and technology integration. By gaining from fruitful contextual analyses and persistently adjusting to developing worldwide patterns, organizations can situate themselves for supported development in the powerful scene of global business.

Choosing the Right Entry Mode

Picking the right passage mode for worldwide market procedure is a basic choice that can fundamentally affect an organization's outcome in global business sectors. The choice interaction includes cautious thought of different variables, including the objective market, industry elements, and the company's assets and capacities.

One of the essential passage modes is trading, which permits organizations to acquaint their items or administrations with global business sectors with somewhat low monetary responsibility and hazard. This can be accomplished through direct exports, in which the business sells directly to customers in other countries, or indirect exports, in which it uses agents or distributors as intermediaries. Sending out is reasonable for organizations with restricted assets and an item that can undoubtedly adjust to unfamiliar business sectors.

On the other hand, permitting and diversifying give an approach to organizations to enter global business sectors without huge capital speculation. Authorizing includes giving unfamiliar substances the freedom to utilize licensed innovation, like licenses or brand names, while diversifying stretches out this idea to incorporate plans of action and functional cycles. When the local partner has a solid understanding of the market and is able to effectively navigate cultural nuances, this entry mode is advantageous.

Joint endeavors and vital unions include coordinated effort with neighborhood accomplices to share dangers, expenses, and ability. This approach is valuable while entering markets with complex administrative conditions or social contrasts. Strategic alliances are partnerships formed without the creation of a new legal entity, whereas joint ventures involve the creation of a new entity in which both partners have a stake. These passage modes permit organizations to use the nearby accomplice's information and assets, working with a smoother market section.

Unfamiliar direct speculation (FDI) is a more significant responsibility, requiring the foundation of completely claimed auxiliaries or securing existing organizations in the objective market. FDI gives more prominent command over activities, yet it implies higher dangers and capital ventures. This section mode is reasonable for organizations looking for long haul presence and a solid serious situation in unfamiliar business sectors.

The decision of passage mode relies upon different elements, and a careful examination is fundamental. Statistical surveying is critical to understanding the objective market's attributes, request, rivalry, and administrative climate. In addition, making an informed decision necessitates evaluating the internal capabilities of the company, such as its technological expertise, financial resources, and managerial capabilities.

Social elements assume a huge part in worldwide market technique. Figuring out nearby traditions, inclinations, and correspondence styles is significant for adjusting items and showcasing techniques. Organizations should lead a careful social investigation to guarantee their contributions line up with the qualities and assumptions for the objective market.

Lawful and administrative contemplations are central in global business. Various nations have shifting guidelines with respect to imports, licensed innovation assurance, and business tasks. To avoid legal issues and ensure compliance with local laws, it is essential to have a comprehensive understanding of these regulations.

Financial variables, for example, trade rates, expansion, and monetary strength, can influence the progress of a worldwide market system. Organizations should assess the monetary states of the objective market to go with informed choices on estimating, monetary preparation, and hazard the board.

Political strength and government arrangements likewise impact the decision of section mode. Business operations may be at risk in politically unstable environments, while favorable government policies may encourage foreign investment. Organizations should evaluate the political scene to moderate likely difficulties and gain by open doors.

Industry-explicit elements ought not be ignored. A few enterprises might be more helpful for specific passage modes because of exceptional qualities and cutthroat designs. Organizations need to consider industry patterns, serious powers, and the particular necessities for progress in the picked market.

picking the right section mode for worldwide market technique is a diverse choice that requires an exhaustive comprehension of outside economic situations and inside hierarchical capacities. Organizations should cautiously evaluate social, lawful, monetary, political, and industry-explicit variables to decide the most appropriate passage mode. Companies can increase their chances of international expansion success and long-term competitiveness by conducting comprehensive market research and strategic analysis.

Joint Ventures, Partnerships, and Acquisitions

In the powerful scene of worldwide business, organizations continually look for procedures to grow their scope, upgrade abilities, and remain serious. Three huge methodologies that associations utilize in this pursuit are Joint Endeavors (JVs), Organizations, and Acquisitions. Each of these strategic initiatives has its own benefits and challenges, making them essential components of a company's global market strategy.

Joint Endeavors (JVs):

In a joint venture, two or more businesses come together to form a new company that shares ownership, risks, and profits. This cooperative exertion permits organizations to use each other's assets, assets, and aptitude to seek after shared objectives.

One of the essential advantages of Joint Endeavors is risk-sharing. Organizations can pool their assets, diminishing monetary weights and spreading functional dangers. This is particularly significant in new or high-risk markets where a solitary element may be reluctant to wander alone. Additionally, joint ventures make it easier for businesses to enter new markets by giving them access to the expertise and networks of their local partners.

However, clear goals, a well-defined governance structure, and careful consideration of partners' compatibility are necessary for successful JVs. Varying administration styles, social subtleties, and clashing objectives can present difficulties. It is fundamental for organizations to concentrate on building trust, adjusting assumptions, and laying out powerful correspondence channels to guarantee the progress of the joint endeavor.

Partnerships:

Organizations are cooperative game plans between organizations that don't be guaranteed to include the production of another substance. All things considered, accomplices keep up with their singular personalities while cooperating towards normal targets.

Organizations can take different structures, like vital unions, circulation arrangements, or exploration coordinated efforts.

One huge benefit of organizations is adaptability. Organizations can participate in unambiguous coordinated efforts custom fitted to their necessities without the intricacies of framing another element. This deftness is especially useful in quickly advancing enterprises where versatility is critical. Companies can also gain access to new markets, technologies, or customer segments through partnerships without having to fully commit to a merger or acquisition.

Nonetheless, the progress of organizations relies on compelling correspondence, common trust, and a common vision. To avoid misunderstandings, businesses must clearly define their roles, responsibilities, and expectations. It is essential to intermittently reevaluate the association's importance and flexibility to guarantee it stays lined up with developing business methodologies.

Acquisitions:

Acquisitions include one organization buying another, prompting an adjustment of proprietorship. A company's growth can be accelerated by this strategic move, which can provide quick access to new markets, technologies, or talent. Acquisitions are much of the time driven by the craving to reinforce serious situating, accomplish cooperative energies, or dispense with contenders.

One of the essential benefits of acquisitions is the speed at which organizations can accomplish vital goals. By getting a current substance, an organization acquires quick admittance to its assets and capacities, saving time contrasted with natural development. Companies gain market power by consolidating their market share and eliminating rivals through acquisitions.

However, there are significant difficulties associated with acquisitions. Social conflicts between the securing and gained substances can affect post-consolidation joining. There is additionally the gamble of misjudging cooperative energies or underrating mix intricacies, prompting sub-standard results. Organizations should lead an exhaustive reasonable level of investment, cautiously plan combination methodologies, and focus on social arrangement to improve the probability of progress.

Worldwide Market Procedure:

Incorporating Joint Endeavors, Organizations, and Acquisitions into a complete worldwide market technique requires a nuanced comprehension of market elements, administrative conditions, and social contemplations. Organizations should adjust these essential drives to their general business objectives, guaranteeing they supplement as opposed to one another. Based on a company's specific goals and challenges, a combination of these approaches is necessary for an effective global market strategy. For example, an organization entering a new and complex market could select a Joint Dare to share dangers and influence neighborhood skill. All the while, framing associations with innovation organizations could assist with upgrading advancement and keep up with intensity. In order to quickly establish a foothold in a crucial market or acquire essential technologies, strategic acquisitions may be pursued.

All in all, Joint Endeavors, Organizations, and Acquisitions are necessary parts of an organization's worldwide market procedure. Each approach offers remarkable benefits and difficulties, and the effective execution of these methodologies requires cautious preparation, an expected level of investment, and flexibility. Organizations that capably explore these essential drives position themselves for supported development, expanded piece of the pie, and improved seriousness in the worldwide commercial center.

Chapter 5 Global Marketing and Branding

Worldwide advertising and marking assume urgent parts in the present interconnected and dynamic business scene. As organizations grow their activities past homegrown lines, the requirement for powerful worldwide promoting systems turns out to be progressively clear. This exposition investigates the critical components of worldwide promoting and marketing, looking at the difficulties and open doors that emerge chasing global achievement.

Worldwide promotion includes thinking up and carrying out showcasing techniques that rise above public limits. It requires a profound comprehension of different societies, monetary frameworks, and customer ways of behaving. One of the crucial parts of fruitful worldwide promotion is the capacity to adjust showcasing messages and missions to resonate with nearby crowds while keeping a predictable worldwide brand personality.

Marking, then again, is the most common way of making a particular and conspicuous personality for an item or organization. For building trust and loyalty in a variety of markets, it is essential to establish a robust and consistent brand in a global setting. A very much created worldwide brand not just conveys the basic beliefs of a business yet in addition fills in as an image of value and unwavering quality.

One of the essential difficulties in worldwide advertising and marking is the social variety present in various business sectors. Social subtleties can altogether influence shopper insights and buying choices. Along these lines, organizations should lead exhaustive statistical surveying to comprehend social contrasts and design their showcasing messages likewise. This might include promoting symbolism, language, and even item elements to line up with nearby inclinations.

One more test lies in exploring the complex administrative conditions of different nations. Every country has its own arrangement of rules and guidelines administering and promoting rehearsals. In order to avoid legal issues and maintain a positive brand image, it is essential to adhere to these regulations. Worldwide advertisers should contribute time and assets to remain informed about global regulations and consistency prerequisites to guarantee consistent activities.

The fast headways in innovation and the ascent of advanced stages have reformed worldwide promoting techniques. Virtual entertainment, web based promoting, and online business have become indispensable parts of worldwide showcasing efforts. Businesses can reach a global audience more effectively and economically by utilizing these digital tools. Nonetheless, it likewise requires a profound comprehension of the computerized scene in each target market.

Notwithstanding social and administrative difficulties, financial elements can essentially influence worldwide showcasing endeavors. Pricing strategies and market positioning can be affected by currency fluctuations, varying levels of economic development, and differences in purchasing power between nations. Worldwide advertisers should cautiously examine financial patterns and adjust their ways to deal with stay cutthroat in different monetary conditions.

Regardless of these difficulties, worldwide advertising and marking offer various open doors for organizations able to put resources into building a global presence. One of the key benefits is the potential for expanded income and portion of the overall industry. By taking advantage of new business sectors, organizations can expand their client base and decrease reliance on unambiguous areas, subsequently moderating dangers related with financial slumps or international vulnerabilities.

Besides, an effective worldwide showcasing procedure can improve a brand's standing and believability. Buyers frequently partner worldwide brands with quality and development, giving an upper hand on the lookout. A positive worldwide brand picture can likewise work with organizations and coordinated efforts with neighborhood organizations, encouraging commonly valuable connections.

Joint efforts with neighborhood powerhouses and vital organizations can be useful assets in worldwide advertising. Working with people or substances that as of now have areas of strength for an objective market can assist with building trust and validity rapidly. Such organizations can give admittance to neighborhood experiences, social subtleties, and laid out networks, empowering more successful promoting efforts.

To succeed in worldwide promotion, organizations should embrace a client driven approach. Understanding the extraordinary necessities and inclinations of interest groups in various areas is fundamental for making important and convincing promoting messages. Key strategies like personalization and localization help brands connect with customers on a deeper level and build customer loyalty.

The significance of flexibility couldn't possibly be more significant in that frame of mind of worldwide advertising. Shopper patterns, market elements, and innovative scenes are ceaselessly advancing. Organizations should be coordinated and responsive, prepared to change their procedures in light of arising patterns and moving customer ways of behaving. For staying ahead of the competition and remaining relevant in the global market, this adaptability is essential.

Taking everything into account, worldwide promoting and marketing are basic parts of the present business methodologies. While difficulties like social variety, administrative intricacies, and financial varieties exist, the open doors for extended reach and expanded memorability make the pursuit advantageous. A nuanced understanding of local markets, a commitment to compliance, and a willingness to change with the times are all necessary for successful global marketing. By embracing these standards, organizations can situate themselves for worldwide achievement and lay out persevering through worldwide brand characters.

Crafting a Global Marketing Strategy

Creating a worldwide showcasing procedure is a complex undertaking that requests cautious thought of different variables. A fruitful methodology includes exploring social subtleties, figuring out different business sectors, and utilizing innovation to make a firm and significant brand presence around the world.

One of the basic components in making a worldwide promoting procedure is statistical surveying. If you want to tailor your message and products to local preferences, it is essential to comprehend the distinctive characteristics of each market. This incorporates concentrating on social standards, shopper ways of behaving, and financial circumstances. Leading careful statistical surveying helps in recognizing open doors and difficulties that might emerge in various districts.

Restriction is a critical part of worldwide promotion. It goes past only deciphering content; it includes adjusting the promoting message to resound with the social setting of each target market. This incorporates language, symbolism, and even item includes. An effective worldwide showcasing technique perceives and regards the variety of the worldwide crowd.

Laying out major areas of strength for a presence worldwide requires consistency. While restriction is essential, keeping a durable brand personality helps in making a bound together picture across different business sectors. Steady visual components, informing, and brand values add to building serious areas of strength for an unmistakable worldwide brand.

It is fundamental in the present interconnected world to Use innovation.

A global marketing strategy's reach and impact can be increased by utilizing digital platforms, social media, and e-commerce channels. Technology not only makes communication easier, but it also makes it possible to market to specific demographics and interests in different regions in a personalized and targeted way.

Web-based entertainment assumes a crucial part in worldwide promotion. Facebook, Instagram, and Twitter are examples of platforms that provide a direct and interactive means of interacting with audiences all over the world. Social media content that is culturally relevant and easy to share can increase brand visibility and create a sense of community among global customers.

Worldwide associations and joint efforts can be key in growing business sector reach. Collaborating with neighborhood organizations or powerhouses can give experiences into the objective market and loan believability to the brand. Organizations additionally consider shared assets and mastery, empowering more compelling entrance into assorted markets.

Versatility is a significant quality in worldwide showcasing. Markets develop, purchaser inclinations change, and international elements can influence business elements. A fruitful worldwide showcasing technique includes persistent checking of market patterns, keeping up to date with administrative changes, and being coordinated in adjusting the promoting approach likewise.

A powerful internet based presence is central for worldwide achievement. A very much planned site that takes care of various dialects and client encounters is indispensable. Web based business capacities ought to be consistent, and the site ought to act as a focal center point for conveying the brand story, values, and item contributions to a worldwide crowd.

Emergency executives are a fundamental piece of worldwide promotion. Occasions like monetary slumps, catastrophic events, or general wellbeing emergencies can fundamentally affect worldwide business sectors. Having alternate courses of action set up and being ready to change methodologies quickly is fundamental for moderating dangers and keeping up with brand flexibility.

When building a global marketing team, a smart move is to invest in culturally intelligent talent. Individuals who are able to navigate cultural differences with sensitivity are necessary for comprehending the nuances of diverse cultures. A different group brings a scope of viewpoints that can add to more powerful worldwide showcasing methodologies.

Measurements and examination give significant bits of knowledge into the presentation of worldwide showcasing endeavors. Checking key execution pointers (KPIs) considers the evaluation of the effect of missions in various business sectors. The refinement of strategies, efficient resource allocation, and overall optimization of the global marketing strategy all benefit from the analysis of data.

creating a worldwide showcasing system is a complex yet fundamental undertaking for organizations trying to flourish in an interconnected world. It includes inside and out research, social responsiveness, innovative incorporation, and flexibility. An effective procedure perceives the variety of worldwide business sectors as well as use it to make a bound together brand personality that resounds with crowds around the world.

Building a Consistent Global Brand Image

Building a steady worldwide brand picture is a multi-layered effort that requires cautious preparation, vital execution, and a profound comprehension of different business sectors. In an interconnected existence where data ventures quickly, keeping up with cognizance across various areas is fundamental for cultivating brand unwaveringly and acknowledgment. This cycle includes adjusting different components, including informing, visual personality, and client experience, to make a brought together brand picture that resounds with crowds around the world.

At the center of a predictable worldwide brand picture is an obvious brand procedure. This entails expressing the brand's purpose, values, and positioning, which ought to be universally applicable while taking into consideration cultural differences. The purpose of a brand is its guiding light and demonstrates its dedication to meeting broader societal requirements. Adjusting this reason to different social qualities is significant to making reverberations on a worldwide scale. For example, a brand stressing supportability might have to adjust its informing to feature explicit natural worries in various districts.

Informing assumes a vital part in building a reliable brand picture across borders. Creating a story that rises above language obstructions while tending to neighborhood responsive qualities requires a nuanced approach. Language nuances, cultural references, and even humor can have a big effect on how people respond to messages. Adjusting information to suit different social settings guarantees that the brand's qualities are imparted successfully without causing accidental mistaken assumptions.

Visual character is one more foundation of worldwide brand consistency. Logos, variety plans, and plan components ought to be firm and effectively conspicuous across different touchpoints. Nevertheless, it is essential to recognize that what resonates in one culture may not have the same impact in another. Adjusting visual components to reflect neighborhood style while keeping up with by and large brand honesty is a fragile difficult exercise. Regardless of where they live, consistency in the brand's visual identity helps customers associate particular characteristics with the company.

Consistency reaches out past advertising materials to include the whole client experience. From item plan to client support, each connection ought to mirror the brand's qualities and standards. Making a consistent and normalized experience cultivates trust and unwavering quality, key parts of serious areas of strength for a brand picture. This requires cautious coordination and arrangement of functional cycles to guarantee consistency in the manner clients see and associate with the brand.

Limitation is a basic part of building a steady worldwide brand picture. While keeping a normalized center, brands should be sufficiently adaptable to adjust to neighborhood inclinations. This includes fitting items, administrations, and showcasing techniques to meet the extraordinary requirements and social subtleties of various areas. For instance, menu things, promoting efforts, or even item elements might be acclimated to line up with nearby preferences and assumptions.

Innovation assumes an instrumental part in accomplishing worldwide brand consistency. Computerized stages give a way to scatter a brand's message quickly, however they likewise require watchful administration to guarantee consistency. Particularly due to the wide range of regional trends and communication styles, social media requires close observation. Brands can quickly adjust to maintain consistency by utilizing technology for data analytics and monitoring. This enables brands to gauge audience reactions in real time.

Legitimate contemplations are vital while building a worldwide brand picture. Brand name assurance, consistency with neighborhood guidelines, and protected innovation freedoms should be carefully made due. A legal error can not only harm the brand's reputation but also cost the company money in litigation. Brands need to explore the intricate snare of global regulations to shield their character and guarantee a predictable picture across borders.

Joint effort across borders is fundamental for worldwide brand consistency. Incorporated brand supervisory crews ought to work intimately with territorial partners to as needs be grasp neighborhood elements and designer procedures. Standard correspondence channels, preparing programs, and cooperative devices work with the trading of bits of knowledge and best practices. This cooperative methodology helps fabricate a mutual perspective of the brand's personality and guarantees that everybody is lined up with the general worldwide technique.

Versatility is a critical quality for keeping a predictable worldwide brand picture. Cultural trends, consumer preferences, and the business landscape are constantly shifting. In order to remain relevant and resonant, brands need to be flexible and regularly reevaluate their strategies. This includes ceaseless observing of market patterns, contender exercises, and arising social movements to proactively change the brand's situation and informing.

fabricating a steady worldwide brand picture is a complex yet imperative endeavor that requests vital reasoning, social responsiveness, and flexibility. A clear cut brand technique, durable informing, and a bound together visual character structure the establishment, while restriction, innovation, lawful contemplations, cooperation, and versatility are the points of support that support worldwide brand consistency. Brands that effectively explore these components make an enduring impression that rises above topographical limits, cultivating areas of strength for shoppers all over the planet.

Chapter 6 Supply Chain and Logistics

In the present interconnected world, the elements of store network and operations assume an urgent part in forming worldwide market procedures. The consistent development of merchandise, data, and capital across borders is fundamental for organizations to flourish in an undeniably aggressive and complex commercial center. This article examines the most important aspects of global market strategy in the supply chain and logistics context, highlighting the issues, opportunities, and best practices that businesses need to take into account.

1. Logistics and Supply Chain Integration A successful global market strategy necessitates the seamless integration of logistics and supply chain operations. This includes upgrading the whole cycle, from obtaining unrefined substances to conveying completed items to purchasers. Blockchain, Artificial Intelligence (AI), and the Internet of Things (IoT) are some of the cutting-edge technologies that businesses frequently use to improve supply chain visibility, efficiency, and traceability.

2. Request Estimating and Arranging
Exact interest gauging is critical for a successful production network. Worldwide market procedure depends on understanding customer inclinations, market patterns, and international factors that might affect interest. Utilizing information investigation and prescient demonstrating assists associations with expecting market moves and adjusting their store network and coordinated factors likewise.

3. Risk The executives in Worldwide Stock Chains
The interconnected idea of worldwide business sectors presents different dangers, including international vulnerabilities, catastrophic events, and production network disturbances. Vigorous gamble the executives systems are fundamental for alleviating these difficulties. Broadening providers, making emergency courses of action,

and utilizing innovation for continuous observing are a portion of the manners in which associations improve flexibility in their production network.

4. Feasible Practices and Moral Stockpile Chains

Lately, there has been a developing emphasis on supportability and moral practices in production networks and coordinated factors. Worldwide market methodologies progressively consolidate harmless to the ecosystem drives, like lessening fossil fuel byproducts and advancing dependable obtaining. Organizations are perceiving that moral stockpile chains line up with buyer values as well as add to long haul outcomes in the worldwide market.

5. Innovation Reception for Effectiveness

The reception of state of the art advances is basic for remaining serious in the worldwide market. Mechanization, advanced mechanics, and computerized reasoning smooth out operations processes, diminishing expenses and expanding effectiveness. Cloud-based stages work with continuous cooperation and data dividing between worldwide production network accomplices.

6. Web based business and Last-Mile Conveyance

The ascent of web based business has changed the scene of store networks and coordinated factors. In order to meet customer expectations for prompt and dependable service, global market strategies now place an emphasis on maximizing last-mile delivery. To improve the effectiveness of last-mile logistics, businesses are investing in novel solutions like autonomous vehicles and drone delivery.

7. A crucial aspect of global market strategy is regulatory compliance and customs management, which involves navigating the intricate web of international regulations and procedures. Organizations should keep up to date with changing exchange strategies, taxes, and consistency prerequisites to stay away from disturbances in the store network. Carrying out powerful traditions the executives rehearses guarantees smooth cross-line development of merchandise.

8. Coordinated effort and Organizations

Coordinated effort is key in the worldwide store network scene. Associations are progressively framing key organizations and collusions with providers, coordinated factors suppliers, and innovation accomplices. These joint efforts upgrade readiness, cultivate development, and make an organization of help to address difficulties in the worldwide market.

9. Consistent Improvement and Flexibility

In a quickly developing worldwide market, versatility is an upper hand. Ceaseless improvement strategies, like Six Sigma and Lean, are broadly embraced to streamline production network processes. It is easier for businesses to deal with uncertainty and seize new opportunities if they foster a culture of innovation and adaptability.

10. Ability Improvement and Preparing

The outcome of a worldwide market procedure vigorously depends on a gifted and proficient labor force. Associations put resources into preparing projects to guarantee that workers have the ability expected to explore the intricacies of the worldwide inventory network and planned operations. For professionals in this field, cross-cultural competence and comprehension of the dynamics of the global market become essential skills.

fostering a strong worldwide market system in production networks and strategies requires an exhaustive methodology that tends to coordination, risk the executives, supportability, innovation reception, and joint effort. Associations that focus on these components and stay nimble in their methodology are better prepared to flourish in the consistently advancing worldwide commercial center. As the world keeps on turning out to be more interconnected, the job of production networks and planned operations in molding worldwide market techniques will just turn out to be more noticeable.

Managing International Supply Chains

In the ever-changing landscape of the global market, managing international supply chains is a challenging and strategic endeavor. As organizations extend their tasks across borders, the complexities of store network the executives become vital in guaranteeing proficiency, cost-adequacy, and responsiveness to advertise requests. In the domain of worldwide market procedure, the compelling administration of global stockpile chains assumes a urgent part in deciding an organization's prosperity.

One of the vital difficulties in overseeing global stockpile chains is the sheer variety of variables that become possibly the most important factor. From various administrative conditions to fluctuating social standards and strategies, organizations should explore a horde of intricacies. Fostering an extensive comprehension of these variables is significant for conceiving a worldwide market procedure that fulfills the needs of the market as well as complies with nearby guidelines and social responsive qualities.

A crucial part of overseeing global stockpile chains is laying out powerful correspondence channels. In a worldwide market situation, where store network accomplices might be dispersed across various landmasses, compelling correspondence turns into the key part of progress. Using cutting edge innovations, for example, cloud-based joint effort apparatuses and ongoing global positioning frameworks, works with consistent correspondence and coordination among different partners in the store network.

Another important aspect of international supply chain management is risk management. Uncertainties in the global market include geopolitical tensions, natural disasters, and economic fluctuations. To relieve these dangers, organizations need to carry out hearty gamble the board procedures that incorporate possibility arranging, expansion of providers, and careful examination of international and financial variables in various locales.

Also, the job of innovation in overseeing global stock chains couldn't possibly be more significant. Data analytics, automation, and artificial intelligence have made it possible to improve supply chain processes. From prescient investigation for request determination to blockchain innovation for improving straightforwardness and detectability, integrating these mechanical progressions engages organizations to smooth out their worldwide stockpile chains.

Finding some kind of harmony between brought together control and decentralized direction is significant in worldwide market methodology. While unified control guarantees consistency and normalization, taking into consideration some level of decentralization engages nearby groups to settle on choices that are receptive to explicit market subtleties. Finding this balance is fundamental for accomplishing functional proficiency without compromising responsiveness to neighborhood market elements.

International supply chain management is receiving more scrutiny in the context of sustainability. Buyers and partners are turning out to be more aware of ecological and social effects, convincing organizations to embrace feasible practices. Integrating eco-accommodating coordinated factors, moral obtaining, and limiting carbon impressions are basic parts of a capable worldwide market system.

Besides, administrative consistency is a vital thought in overseeing global stockpile chains. Exploring different administrative structures requires a fastidious way to deal with guarantee adherence to regulations and norms in each working locale. Organizations should keep up to date with changes in guidelines and proactively change their store network cycles to stay consistent and keep away from lawful confusions.

Cooperation with neighborhood accomplices is a vital part of overseeing global inventory chains really. Building solid associations with providers, merchants, and different partners in various districts encourages a feeling of trust and improves the deftness of the store network. Laying out nearby organizations likewise gives bits of knowledge into local market elements, assisting organizations with fitting their worldwide market procedure to explicit requirements.

overseeing worldwide stockpile chains with regards to worldwide market procedure requests a comprehensive and versatile methodology. To ensure the smooth movement of goods and services across borders, businesses must address a variety of obstacles, including utilizing technology and navigating various regulatory environments. Finding some kind of harmony among normalization and limitation, embracing manageability, and encouraging joint effort with nearby accomplices are fundamental components in the mind boggling embroidered artwork of worldwide store network the board in the worldwide market.

Efficient Global Logistics Planning

Proficient worldwide strategies arranging is significant for organizations working on a worldwide scale. It is essential to optimize the movement of goods from manufacturing to the final consumer in an interconnected world where markets transcend borders. Strategic decision-making, the application of cutting-edge technology, and a thorough comprehension of the intricate dynamics of the supply chain are all required for this intricate procedure.

One critical part of proficient worldwide strategies arranging is store network perceivability. Having constant perceivability into the whole production network permits organizations to expect interruptions, recognize bottlenecks, and answer quickly to changes. Trend setting innovations like RFID, IoT sensors, and blockchain assume a critical part in accomplishing this straightforwardness. These innovations give exact, modern data about the area and state of items as they travel through the production network.

Additionally, utilizing information investigation is fundamental for powerful coordinated operations arranging. Dissecting verifiable information assists in anticipating, requesting, enhancing stock levels, and pursuing informed choices. Companies can align their logistics strategies in response to anticipated future trends and demand patterns thanks to predictive analytics. This information driven approach upgrades by and large proficiency by decreasing overload or stockouts and limiting pointless transportation costs.

Worldwide coordinated factors arranging likewise requires a strong transportation system. Picking the correct method of transportation, whether it be air, ocean, street, or rail, relies upon factors like expense, travel time, and the idea of the products being shipped. For long-distance shipments, intermodal transportation, which combines multiple modes, can be a cost-effective option. Furthermore, course streamlining utilizing GPS and progressing steering calculations lessens travel time and fuel utilization, adding to both expense investment funds and natural maintainability.

Joint effort is one more basic component in productive coordinated factors arranging. Lying areas of strength for out with providers, transporters, and outsider coordinated factors suppliers encourages a consistent progression of data and assets. Cooperative preparation and determining guarantee that all partners are adjusted, lessening the gamble of miscommunication and further developing general store network effectiveness.

Compliance with international regulations and customs procedures is crucial in global logistics. Exploring the intricacies of different traditions necessities and exchange guidelines requests careful preparation.

Businesses can avoid delays, fines, and other complications that may result from noncompliance by employing experts in international trade and customs laws.

Warehousing and dispersion focuses likewise assume a critical part in worldwide strategies arranging. Moving warehouses strategically closer to important markets can shorten transit times and lower transportation costs. Automated warehouse management systems reduce operational errors, speed up order fulfillment, and improve accuracy. Besides, taking on a "in the nick of time" stock methodology guarantees that merchandise are accessible while required, limiting overabundance stock holding costs.

Innovation keeps on reforming worldwide strategies. By analyzing massive amounts of data in real time, algorithms for artificial intelligence (AI) and machine learning (ML) improve decision-making processes. Mechanization, including independent vehicles and automated distribution center frameworks, smoothes out activities and decreases the dependence on difficult work. Last-mile delivery using drones and autonomous vehicles is becoming increasingly researched due to their faster and less expensive alternatives.

Notwithstanding the advantages of mechanical headways, online protection is a developing worry in worldwide coordinated factors. As strategy frameworks become more interconnected and dependent on advanced innovations, safeguarding delicate information from digital dangers is central. Carrying out vigorous online protection measures, including encryption, secure organizations, and normal reviews, is crucial for defending the trustworthiness and secrecy of coordinated factors information.

effective global logistics planning is a complex undertaking that necessitates a comprehensive strategy. From utilizing trend setting innovations to encouraging cooperation and guaranteeing consistency with worldwide guidelines, organizations should explore an intricate scene to upgrade their inventory network. By focusing on store network perceivability, information examination, transportation techniques, cooperation, consistency, warehousing, and embracing rising advancements, organizations can accomplish an upper hand in the worldwide market.

Chapter 9 Financial Planning and Risk Management

A successful strategy for the global market relies heavily on financial planning and risk management. In the consistently developing scene of the worldwide market, organizations face complex difficulties and vulnerabilities that require vital premonition and a distinct way to deal with monetary administration.

The foundation of any successful global market strategy is financial planning. It includes the precise assignment of assets to meet an association's goals while considering the vulnerabilities related with the worldwide market. Budgeting, forecasting, and capital allocation are all parts of a comprehensive financial plan that show a path to achieving both short-term and long-term objectives.

With regards to the worldwide market system, understanding and it is vital to adjust to assorted monetary conditions. This necessitates a thorough examination of currency fluctuations, geopolitical factors, and global economic trends. To mitigate risks associated with economic downturns, trade tensions, and other external factors that have the potential to affect the global market, financial planning ought to incorporate contingency measures.

Risk the executives, firmly interweaved with monetary preparation, is the most common way of distinguishing, surveying, and relieving possible dangers to an association's targets. In the worldwide market, dangers can appear in different structures, including cash risk, international gamble, administrative gamble, and market unpredictability. A powerful gamble the executives procedure is fundamental to explore these difficulties and shield the monetary strength of the association.

Cash risk is a conspicuous worry in the worldwide market, given the fluctuating trade rates between various monetary forms. Organizations participating in worldwide exchange should cautiously oversee openness to cash chance to forestall antagonistic consequences for benefit. This might include utilizing monetary instruments, for example, forward agreements or choices to fence against money changes.

International gamble adds one more layer of intricacy to worldwide market technique. Political flimsiness, exchange pressures, and provincial contentions can essentially influence business tasks. Scenario analysis and stress testing should be included in a comprehensive risk management plan to evaluate the potential impact of geopolitical events on the organization's financial performance.

Administrative gamble is a consistent thought in the worldwide market, with changing lawful and consistent prerequisites across various districts. Complying with global guidelines while exploring neighborhood regulations requests a proactive and versatile methodology. Monetary arranging ought to represent possible changes in guidelines and apportion assets to guarantee consistence.

Market unpredictability, impacted by variables like financial pointers, mechanical headways, and purchaser conduct, represents a ceaseless test in the worldwide market. Organizations should execute risk moderation techniques, including enhancement of portfolios and the utilization of subordinates, to explore market changes and protect monetary strength.

Finding some kind of harmony among hazard and award is fundamental in worldwide market technique. While the risk the board expects to relieve likely dangers, it shouldn't smother development or upset the quest for vital open doors. Financial planning needs to be in line with the company's strategic goals and tolerance for risk so that it can react quickly to changes in the market.

In the time of computerized change, mechanical progressions carry the two valuable open doors and dangers to worldwide market players. Embracing development while dealing with the related online protection chances is critical. Investing in robust cybersecurity measures, which safeguard confidential financial data and maintain stakeholders' trust, should be prioritized in financial planning.

The combination of natural, social, and administration (ESG) contemplations further entangles worldwide market methodology. Organizations are under expanding strain to show moral and reasonable practices. Monetary arranging ought to consolidate ESG measurements, mirroring a pledge to dependable corporate citizenship and lining up with the assumptions for financial backers and shoppers.

monetary preparation and hazard the executives are basic parts of an effective worldwide market procedure. A very much created monetary arrangement gives a guide to asset distribution and objective fulfillment, while compelling gamble the board shields against the vulnerabilities intrinsic in the worldwide market. By exploring cash gambles, international difficulties, administrative intricacies, and market unpredictability, organizations can situate themselves for reasonable development and flexibility in the always changing worldwide scene.

Budgeting for Global Expansion

Planning for worldwide extension is a basic part of making arrangements for organizations intending to broaden their tasks past homegrown lines. This complex interaction includes careful monetary preparation, risk evaluation, and an intensive comprehension of the different financial scenes across target markets. In this conversation, we will dive into key contemplations and techniques associated with planning for worldwide development.

Conducting an extensive market analysis is one of the initial steps in the budgeting process. This includes assessing potential business sectors in light of elements like monetary dependability, administrative conditions, and social subtleties. To create a precise budget, it is essential to comprehend the distinct challenges and opportunities presented by each market. An exhaustive market investigation can assist with recognizing possible dangers and moderate them through informed monetary preparation.

When potential business sectors are distinguished, organizations should evaluate the expenses related with market passage. This incorporates costs connected with legitimate consistency, permitting, and laying out an actual presence, like workplaces or assembling offices. Costs associated with adapting products or services to local preferences and standards must also be taken into account by businesses. Organizations can avoid financial surprises and strategically allocate resources by accurately estimating these entry costs.

Cash vacillations represent a huge gamble in worldwide development. Organizations should consider the likely effect of cash swapping scale changes on their spending plan. Executing risk the executives procedures, for example, utilizing monetary instruments like forward agreements, can assist with alleviating money gambles and give greater soundness to the planning system.

Ability securing and labor force the board are pivotal parts of worldwide extension. The venture's success is aided by an understanding of the local labor market, the hiring of skilled professionals, and the provision of appropriate training. Recruitment expenses, employee benefits, and ongoing training initiatives should all be included in the budget. Guaranteeing an exceptional and socially different labor force improves flexibility and proficiency in worldwide business sectors.

Store network coordinated factors assume a vital part in worldwide extension, influencing the two expenses and functional productivity. Organizations need to assess transportation costs, import/trade obligations, and capacity costs. The supply chain can be optimized and costs reduced by forming strategic partnerships with local distributors and suppliers. A strong and effective production network is fundamental for fulfilling client needs and keeping up with seriousness in new business sectors.

Consistence with nearby guidelines is a basic part of worldwide extension. Organizations should apportion assets for legitimate advice to explore complex administrative conditions. This incorporates figuring out charge regulations, exchange guidelines, and industry-explicit consistency necessities. Inability to conform to nearby guidelines can prompt lawful issues and monetary punishments, highlighting the significance of a clear cut financial plan for legitimate and administrative undertakings.

Putting resources into the innovation foundation is fundamental for consistent worldwide activities. Planning for strong IT frameworks, network safety measures, and versatile stages guarantees that the association can adjust to the mechanical scene of various business sectors. This incorporates contemplations for confining advanced resources, following information insurance guidelines, and coordinating innovation arrangements that line up with local inclinations.

The development of a brand and marketing strategies are crucial to successful global expansion. Organizations need to allot assets for statistical surveying, publicizing, and special exercises customized to each target market. Social awareness is vital in promoting efforts that reverberate with assorted crowds. A thoroughly examined showcasing spending plan can fundamentally influence brand perceivability and client procurement in new business sectors.

Budgeting for global expansion relies heavily on contingency planning. A portion of a company's budget should be set aside for emergencies and challenges that come up unexpectedly. Whether it's international precariousness, catastrophic events, or startling business sector shifts, having a possibility reserve gives the adaptability to explore vulnerabilities without compromising the by and large monetary soundness of the extension drive.

A comprehensive and strategic approach is required when budgeting for global expansion. To come up with a budget that is both accurate and attainable, businesses need to take into account a wide range of factors, including currency risks, talent acquisition, compliance, market analysis, and entry costs. By tending to these contemplations, associations can situate themselves for outcome in the dynamic and cutthroat scene of worldwide business sectors.

Mitigating Financial Risks in International Markets

A crucial component of developing a successful strategy for the global market is reducing the financial risks that exist in international markets. As organizations grow past homegrown lines, they open themselves to different vulnerabilities, including money variances, international occasions, and monetary insecurities. Successfully exploring these difficulties requires an extensive methodology that consolidates risk evaluation, vital preparation, and monetary instruments.

A thorough risk assessment is an essential component of mitigating financial risks on international markets. Understanding the potential dangers related with a specific market or district is fundamental for fostering a powerful worldwide market methodology. Cultural factors, regulatory environments, political stability, and economic conditions are all examined in this assessment. For example, an organization working in a politically unpredictable district might confront higher dangers contrasted with a steady and deeply grounded market. By recognizing and dissecting these dangers, associations can pursue informed choices and designer their systems as needs be.

Money risk is a main pressing issue for organizations that take part in worldwide exchange. The profitability of transactions can be significantly affected by fluctuations in exchange rates. To moderate money risk, organizations frequently utilize monetary instruments like supporting methodologies. Forward agreements, choices, and money trades are normal instruments utilized to safeguard against unfriendly cash developments. By securing in return rates ahead of time, organizations can more readily anticipate their future incomes and decrease the effect of cash unpredictability on their primary concern.

Political and administrative dangers are inborn in global business sectors. Changes in government arrangements, economic accords, or neighborhood guidelines can influence organizations working universally. To address these dangers, organizations ought to remain informed about political turns of events and keep up with adaptability in their tasks. Differentiating tasks across various districts can likewise assist with relieving the effect of unfavorable political occasions in a particular area.

Monetary vulnerabilities, including expansion, loan cost variances, and financial slumps, represent extra difficulties in worldwide business sectors. Leading careful statistical surveying and remaining receptive to financial pointers can support expecting and overseeing monetary dangers. Carrying out adaptable valuing systems and changing creation and conveyance plans because of monetary movements can improve an organization's versatility notwithstanding financial vulnerabilities.

Financial risks on global markets can be mitigated through strategic planning. Fostering a distinct worldwide market technique requires adjusting business targets to gamble with resistance and economic situations. Organizations ought to lay out clear objectives, evaluate their serious situation, and persistently screen and adjust their procedures in light of developing business sector elements.

Enhancement is a basic methodology for risk moderation. Spreading activities across assorted markets diminishes dependence on any single market, limiting the effect of territorial explicit difficulties. By entering markets with differing financial circumstances and chance profiles, organizations can make a stronger worldwide portfolio.

Another effective method for reducing risks is to work together with partners in the local community. Nearby accomplices frequently have important experiences into the subtleties of the market, administrative scene, and buyer conduct. A company's ability to navigate complex environments and mitigate risks associated with unfamiliar markets can be improved through partnerships with established organizations.

Compelling correspondence and relationship with the executives are basic parts of an effective worldwide market technique. Building solid associations with partners, including providers, clients, and nearby specialists, can work with better gamble the board. Open correspondence channels empower associations to answer rapidly to arising moves and team up with partners to track down practical arrangements.

Mechanical headways likewise assume a critical part in moderating monetary dangers in global business sectors. Enhancing risk assessment capabilities can be made possible by making use of cutting-edge financial technologies like artificial intelligence and predictive analytics. Businesses can now develop proactive strategies to address potential risks in real time thanks to these tools.

moderating monetary dangers in worldwide business sectors is a complex undertaking that requires a blend of hazard evaluation, key preparation, and proactive administration. By understanding the remarkable difficulties related with worldwide activities and carrying out vigorous gamble alleviation procedures, organizations can situate themselves for feasible progress in the dynamic and interconnected universe of global business sectors.

Chapter 10 Technology and Digital Presence

In the speedy and interconnected universe of business, utilizing innovation and laying out a powerful computerized presence have become basic parts of worldwide market methodology. The computerized scene has changed how organizations work, impart, and contend on a worldwide scale. Organizations navigating the dynamic global market face new opportunities and challenges as a result of this shift, which has also reshaped traditional business models.

Global Markets and Technology's Development:

Throughout the course of recent years, mechanical headways play had a vital impact in molding the worldwide market scene. The ascent of the web, portable advances, and refined information investigation has worked with consistent correspondence and coordinated effort across borders. Organizations are not generally restricted by geological limits, and innovation has turned into the impetus for growing their scope and impact around the world.

Computerized Change as an Essential Objective:

Companies are increasingly accepting digital transformation as a strategic necessity in order to gain a competitive advantage. This includes the combination of advanced innovations into all parts of business tasks, on a very basic level changing how organizations convey worth to clients. From inventory network the executives to client care, advanced change pervades each feature of the worldwide market procedure.

Online business and Worldwide Reach:

One of the most apparent effects of innovation on worldwide market methodology is the multiplication of web based business. With the appearance of online stages and secure installment entryways, organizations can now arrive at buyers in far off corners of the world. E-commerce not only makes international trade easier, but it also lets smaller businesses compete globally, leveling the playing field and making the global market more open to everyone.

Making decisions based on data:

The computerized time has introduced a period of information overflow. Organizations currently approach huge measures of data created by client corporations, exchanges, and market patterns. Organizations are able to make decisions based on data that are well-informed when they are able to harness and analyze this data. Prescient examination and man-made consciousness empower organizations to expect market patterns, improve tasks, and tweak their contributions to meet the different requirements of a worldwide client base.

Virtual Entertainment and Brand Perceivability:

As a direct means by which businesses can interact with their target audience, social media platforms have emerged as an essential component of global market strategies. Fabricating and keeping areas of strength for a media presence isn't just about promoting items yet additionally about developing a brand character. Organizations that effectively explore web-based entertainment can upgrade their image perceivability, interface with clients on an individual level, and even location worldwide emergencies or difficulties quickly.

Problems in the Global Digital Arena:

Technology presents challenges in the global market as well as enormous opportunities. Network protection dangers, administrative intricacies, and social contrasts can present obstacles for organizations planning to lay out a computerized presence on a worldwide scale. Finding some kind of harmony among normalization and restriction is critical, as need might arise to fit their methodologies to the exceptional qualities of each market while keeping a durable worldwide personality.

The Function of Mobile Technology:
The broad reception of versatile innovations has additionally sped up the computerized change of worldwide business sectors. Versatile applications and responsive sites empower organizations to arrive at purchasers on their favored gadgets, giving a consistent and customized client experience. Versatile advances upgrade openness as well as work with ongoing correspondence, making it more straightforward for organizations to draw in with clients and answer market changes immediately.

Arising Advancements Molding What's to come:
Emerging trends like the Internet of Things (IoT), blockchain, and 5G stand to reshape global market strategies as technology advances. IoT interfaces gadgets and empowers continuous checking and control, upsetting businesses like assembling and operations. Blockchain guarantees straightforward and secure exchanges, cultivating trust in worldwide transactions. The rollout of 5G organizations guarantees quicker and

more solid correspondence, opening additional opportunities for advancement and network.

Adjusting to Mechanical Disturbances:

Effective worldwide market systems expect versatility to innovative disturbances. Organizations should remain lithe and embrace development to remain on top of things. The people who neglect to adjust risk becoming outdated in a climate where mechanical headways happen at an exceptional speed. Persistent interest in innovative work, remaining informed about industry patterns, and encouraging a culture of development are fundamental for long haul progress in the computerized worldwide field.

innovation and advanced presence are fundamental to the outcome of worldwide market methodologies. The interconnected idea of the cutting edge business scene requires a proactive way to deal with utilizing innovation for extension, effectiveness, and client commitment. As organizations explore the intricacies of the worldwide market, embracing computerized change, tackling information, and remaining sensitive to arising innovations are basic for keeping an upper hand. The associations that effectively coordinate innovation into their worldwide methodologies won't just make due however flourish in the consistently developing computerized time.

Leveraging Technology for Global Reach

In today's interconnected world, businesses, organizations, and individuals must utilize technology for global reach. Not only have advanced technologies made communication easier, but they have also opened up previously unheard-of opportunities for reaching a global audience. In this period of computerized change, organizations that tackle the force of innovation can expand their impact past geological limits, taking advantage of new business sectors and encouraging joint effort on a worldwide scale.

One of the key ways innovation empowers worldwide reach is through the web. The Internet fills in as an immense stage for data trade, correspondence, and business. It is possible for businesses to establish an online presence and reach potential clients on every continent. Internet business stages have democratized retail, permitting even independent ventures to feature and offer their items to a worldwide client base. This shift has re-imagined customary plans of action, giving open doors to development that were once unfathomable.

Web-based entertainment stages assume an essential part in extending worldwide reach. Platforms like Facebook, Instagram, Twitter, and LinkedIn provide unparalleled reach and engagement with billions of users worldwide. On a global scale, organizations can create targeted content, connect with their audience, and raise brand awareness. Web-based entertainment goes about as a useful asset for showcasing, empowering organizations to fit their messages to explicit socioeconomics and locales, in this way boosting their effect.

The global business landscape has been further transformed by the rise of cloud computing. Teams scattered across the globe can seamlessly collaborate and share data using cloud technology. This works with continuous correspondence, project the board, and asset designation, separating geological obstructions. The capacity to get to information and applications from anyplace improves proficiency and spryness, giving associations an upper hand in the worldwide market.

Man-made consciousness (artificial intelligence) and AI (ML) are instrumental in computerizing processes and customizing encounters on a worldwide scale. Organizations influence computer based intelligence to examine immense measures of information, acquiring bits of knowledge into customer conduct and market patterns. This empowers them to fit items and administrations to meet the different necessities of a worldwide crowd. Furthermore, artificial intelligence fueled language interpretation administrations span correspondence holes, working with connections among people and organizations from various semantic foundations.

The Web of Things (IoT) has changed businesses by associating gadgets and empowering them to impart and share information. This interconnectedness has broad ramifications for worldwide organizations, especially in strategies and store network. IoT gadgets give constant following of shipments, screen stock levels, and improve production network processes, guaranteeing consistent procedure on a worldwide scale. This not only makes things run more smoothly, but it also saves money and makes customers happier as a whole.

The technologies of virtual reality (VR) and augmented reality (AR) provide immersive experiences that can take place anywhere. Organizations can lead virtual gatherings, introductions, and item showings, disposing of the requirement for actual presence. This saves time and assets as well as opens up doors for worldwide joint effort and development. VR and AR applications stretch out past business, impacting areas like training and medical care by giving remote learning and telemedicine arrangements.

Blockchain innovation, known at first for its job in digital money, has tracked down applications in guaranteeing straightforwardness and security in worldwide exchanges. Brilliant agreements on blockchain stages work with trustless arrangements, decreasing the requirement for middle people in global dealings. Cross-border transactions become more reliable and effective as a result of this, which not only streamlines procedures but also reduces the likelihood of fraud.

Worldwide reach likewise stretches out to the domain of schooling, where web based gaining stages empower understudies from around the world to get to excellent training. Innovation has made it feasible for famous establishments to bring courses and degrees to a worldwide crowd, democratizing training and encouraging a culture of ceaseless learning on a worldwide scale.

In any case, while innovation opens ways to open doors worldwide, it likewise brings difficulties that require conscious thought. Network protection becomes principal as associations manage delicate information and data on a worldwide scale. Guaranteeing the security and assurance of client information is vital to keeping up with trust in an interconnected world.

Besides, the computerized partition stays a huge obstacle in accomplishing genuine worldwide reach. Aberrations in web access and mechanical foundation frustrate people and networks from completely partaking in the computerized economy. Overcoming this issue requires deliberate endeavors from state run administrations, organizations, and global associations to guarantee that the advantages of innovation are available to all.

utilizing innovation for worldwide reach has turned into a characterizing factor in the progress of organizations and associations. The interconnectedness worked with the web, virtual entertainment, distributed computing, computer based intelligence, IoT, VR, AR, blockchain, and online instruction has reshaped conventional standards.

The adoption of these technologies not only broadens the reach of the market but also encourages international cooperation, creativity, and cultural exchange. As we explore the intricacies of an interconnected world, it is essential to saddle innovation mindfully, addressing modes and guaranteeing inclusivity to understand the capability of worldwide reach in the advanced age genuinely.

Establishing a Strong Online Presence

Laying out major areas of strength for a presence is significant in the present interconnected worldwide market. In a period where computerized corporations rule business scenes, a strong web-based presence can be a unique advantage for organizations looking to grow their range and impact. A clear cut worldwide market technique is fundamental to explore the intricacies of different business sectors and interface with a wide crowd. This article investigates key parts and procedures for building serious areas of strength for a presence in the worldwide market.

Figuring out the Worldwide Scene

Prior to plunging into the particulars of online presence, it's fundamental to comprehend the worldwide business scene. Various locales have one of a kind societies, inclinations, and guidelines that can fundamentally influence market section and achievement. Leading intensive statistical surveying is central to recognize ideal interest groups, contenders, and arising patterns. This knowledge shapes the establishment for a custom-made worldwide market system.

Creating a Comprehensive Website

The website of a company is frequently the first point of contact for potential clients. It fills in as a virtual retail facade and ought to mirror the brand personality reliably across various societies. The site ought to be easy to understand, improved for web search tools, and open in numerous dialects. Users around the world will have a smooth experience thanks to a responsive design that works with a variety of devices.

Utilizing Web-based Entertainment Stages

Web-based entertainment has turned into an amazing asset for worldwide effort. Stages like Facebook, Twitter, Instagram, and LinkedIn offer assorted channels to draw in with crowds. Fitting substance to suit every stage and its client socioeconomics is pivotal. Predictable and significant collaboration via online entertainment encourages a feeling of local area and fabricates brand reliability across borders.

Executing Site design improvement (Search engine optimization)

Powerful Web optimization rehearses to upgrade an organization's perceivability on web indexes, driving natural traffic to its site. Watchword improvement, excellent substance creation, and backlink building are essential parts of an effective Website optimization technique. Restricted Website design enhancement endeavors can additionally improve online presence for explicit districts, guaranteeing that the organization positions high in important ventures.

Using Online business Stages
Online business stages give an immediate channel to organizations to universally arrive at clients. Stages like Shopify, Amazon, and Alibaba work with global exchanges and delivery. Adjusting item postings, installment choices, and transportation subtleties to take care of assorted markets is fundamental. Giving restricted client assistance can likewise upgrade the general shopping experience for worldwide clients.

Participating in Satisfied Advertising
Content promoting stays an integral asset for laying out experts in the worldwide market. Making important, pertinent, and shareable substance helps position an organization as an industry chief. Blog entries, articles, recordings, and infographics can be customized to address the particular requirements and interests of different crowds. Over time, creating consistent content increases credibility and trust.

Executing Multilingual and Multicultural Showcasing
Language is a basic method of calculating successful correspondence. Offering content in different dialects exhibits a promise to draw in with different crowds. Additionally, it is essential to have an understanding of cultural nuances in order to avoid unintentional errors that could turn away potential clients. A multicultural way to

deal with promoting guarantees that missions resound with various segment gatherings.

Bridling the Force of Powerhouse Advertising

Powerhouses can assume a huge part in growing a brand's span worldwide. Joining forces with powerhouses who have major areas of strength for an in target markets can give admittance to new crowds. Credible joint efforts that line up with the powerhouse's qualities and the brand's message are bound to resound with their adherents.

Embracing Diverse Correspondence

Clear and powerful correspondence is at the center of an effective worldwide market methodology. Embracing diverse correspondence includes understanding social contrasts in correspondence styles, behavior, and strategic approaches. Fitting showcasing messages to reverberate with social qualities can make a brand more interesting and interesting to different crowds.

Checking and Adjusting Techniques

The worldwide market is dynamic, and procedures should advance to remain applicable. Consistently checking key execution pointers (KPIs), client criticism, and market patterns permits organizations to successfully adjust their systems. Adaptability and an eagerness to emphasize on approaches are fundamental for long haul progress in the steadily changing worldwide business scene.

Laying out serious areas of strength for a presence in the worldwide market requires a comprehensive and versatile methodology. From a very much planned site and powerful Website design enhancement to online entertainment commitment and diverse correspondence, every part assumes a vital part. A thorough comprehension of target markets, combined with a pledge to progressing improvement, positions organizations for outcome in the interconnected and serious worldwide commercial center. By embracing these techniques, organizations can fabricate enduring associations with clients all over the planet and flourish in the computerized age.

Chapter 11
Case Studies

Worldwide market systems are a basic part of business development, expecting organizations to adjust their ways to deal with various districts and markets. A few contextual investigations offer bits of knowledge into effective and testing worldwide market systems.

1. The McDonald's Company: Worldwide Normalization versus Limitation

McDonald's is an exemplary illustration of an organization that effectively carried out a worldwide market procedure while adjusting normalization and limitation. By keeping up with center menu things universally while adjusting to nearby preferences, McDonald's successfully entered assorted markets.

2. Coca-Cola's Worldwide Marking Methodology

Coca-Cola has reliably applied a worldwide marking methodology, stressing a bound together brand picture around the world. In spite of confronting social contrasts, the organization's emphasis on keeping a durable worldwide brand has added to its outcome in different business sectors.

3. Huawei's Worldwide Development
Huawei's worldwide development gives a contextual analysis in how a Chinese tech organization explored global business sectors. Challenges included administrative issues, international pressures, and social contrasts, accentuating the significance of adjusting procedures to assorted conditions.

4. IKEA: Adapting to Local Preferences IKEA's success in international markets is due to its capacity to combine a standard product line with an awareness of local preferences. The company shows how important flexibility is in global strategy by tailoring its offerings to different cultural preferences and home lifestyles.

5. Apple's Entry into the Chinese Market
Apple's entry into the Chinese market was hampered by local rivals, complicated regulations, and consumer preferences. The case demonstrates how crucial it is to comprehend the distinctive dynamics of a target market and make appropriate strategic adjustments.

6. Settle's Multi-Image Technique
Settle's worldwide market technique includes dealing with a broad arrangement of brands, each custom fitted to neighborhood markets. This

approach permits the organization to meet assorted buyer inclinations while profiting from economies of scale underway and appropriation.

7. Amazon's Worldwide Online business Strength

Amazon's worldwide achievement is credited to its imaginative online business procedures and versatility. The organization fits its contributions to address the issues of various business sectors, exhibiting the significance of innovation and coordinated operations in executing an effective worldwide system.

8. Unilever's Supportable Plan of action

Unilever's worldwide market procedure centers around manageability and corporate social obligation. By adjusting its items to ecological and social worries, Unilever has engaged a more extensive shopper base, underscoring the developing significance of moral contemplations in worldwide business.

9. Toyota's Worldwide Inventory network The executives

Toyota's effective worldwide store network, the board is a contextual investigation in enhancing tasks across borders. Lean manufacturing principles and just-in-time inventory systems help the business stay ahead of the competition in a variety of markets.

10. Microsoft's Worldwide Programming Restriction

Microsoft's methodology of confining programming items for various dialects and social settings has been critical to its worldwide achievement. This contextual analysis highlights the significance of adjusting items to phonetic and social subtleties in global business sectors.

These contextual analyses feature the assorted methodologies organizations take in making and executing worldwide market techniques. From adjusting normalization and limitation to exploring administrative difficulties and embracing supportability, effective worldwide systems require a nuanced comprehension of each market's exceptional elements. As organizations keep on growing universally, gaining from these contextual investigations becomes fundamental for remaining serious in an interconnected world.

Real-world Examples of Successful Global Market Expansion

Many businesses make the strategic decision to enter international markets in order to achieve growth, diversify their revenue streams, and reach new customer bases. Effective worldwide market development requires an intensive comprehension of different societies, administrative conditions, and buyer ways of behaving. The following are a few genuine instances of organizations that have explored these difficulties really, showing effective worldwide development.

McDonald's: Worldwide Cheap Food Strength

McDonald's is a perfect representation of effective worldwide market development. The organization, beginning in the US, has extended its tasks to more than 100 nations, fitting its menu to nearby preferences while keeping a predictable worldwide brand. The transformation of menu items, for example, the presentation of the McPaneer Royale in India to oblige vegan inclinations, exhibits the significance of social awareness in global extension.

Toyota: Driving Worldwide Extension

Toyota, the Japanese car goliath, has decisively extended its activities around the world, becoming one of the biggest and best vehicle makers universally. By figuring out territorial inclinations, adjusting item contributions, and laying out neighborhood creation offices, Toyota has really entered assorted markets. The company's success in maintaining a strong global presence can be attributed to its dedication to quality and innovation.

Samsung: Hardware on a Worldwide Scale

South Korean aggregate Samsung has effectively extended its hardware business around the world. Through steady development, item expansion, and an emphasis on quality, Samsung has turned into a key part in the worldwide shopper hardware market. The organization's capacity to adjust its showcasing techniques to suit various districts while keeping a durable brand picture has been significant to its prosperity.

Alibaba: Web based business Domain

Alibaba, the Chinese web based business goliath, has shown noteworthy worldwide extension, basically through its foundation like AliExpress. By associating Chinese producers with customers around the world, Alibaba has taken advantage of the developing interest for web based shopping. The organization's prosperity isn't simply credited to its immense item contributions yet additionally to how its might interpret cross-line exchange guidelines and obligation to giving secure installment frameworks.

Unilever: Purchaser Products Across Mainlands

Unilever, a global buyer merchandise organization, has effectively extended its impression across landmasses. Unilever caters its offerings to local tastes by offering a wide range of food, household, and personal care products. The securing of nearby brands, like India's Hindustan Unilever Restricted, has additionally fortified its presence in unambiguous locales.

Netflix: Streaming Around the world

Netflix, an American real time feature, has made worldwide progress by adjusting its substance to different social preferences. Netflix has built a sizable global subscriber base by investing in original content from various regions and providing recommendations for local content. The organization's worldwide extension system includes figuring out the subtleties of diversion inclinations in different nations, considering a customized client experience.

IKEA: Level Stuffed Furnishings, Worldwide Achievement

Swedish furniture retailer IKEA has effectively extended its activities internationally by offering reasonable, useful, and in vogue furniture. IKEA's level stuffed furniture model decreases transportation costs as well as lines up with worldwide supportability patterns. The organization's obligation to nearby obtaining and adjusting its item reach to fit different market requests has added to its outcome in assorted districts.

Coca-Cola: The Worldwide Drink Symbol

Coca-Cola, a famous American refreshment organization, has kept up with its worldwide strength by adjusting its promoting procedures to nearby societies. Through essential associations, restricted promoting efforts, and item development, Coca-Cola has imbued itself in the texture of different social orders around the world. The organization's capacity to keep a reliable brand picture while regarding neighborhood inclinations has been vital to its getting through progress.

Huawei: Chinese Tech Monster

Huawei, a Chinese worldwide innovation organization, has effectively extended its presence in the worldwide broadcast communications and cell phone markets. Notwithstanding confronting international difficulties, Huawei's emphasis on innovative work, combined with serious evaluation, has permitted it to acquire a huge piece of the pie in different nations. The company's global success can be attributed to its dedication to innovation and investment in 5G technology.

Starbucks: Espresso Culture Around the world

Starbucks, starting in the US, has turned into a worldwide café chain by adjusting its contributions to take special care of neighborhood tastes and inclinations. The organization has effectively explored social contrasts by integrating area explicit things into its menu while keeping up with the center Starbucks experience. Starbucks' accentuation on making an inviting climate has resounded with purchasers around the world, adding to its global achievement.
effective worldwide market extension includes a mix of flexibility, social comprehension, and vital navigation. Organizations that have successfully expanded internationally, as featured by the models above, focus on limitation, development, and a guarantee to meeting the special necessities of different business sectors. These examples of overcoming adversity give significant bits of knowledge to organizations looking to leave on their own worldwide extension ventures.

CONCLUSION

Key Strategies on Looking Ahead to Future Global Business Trends

Exploring the future worldwide business scene requires an essential methodology that envelops different key patterns and markets. The powerful idea of the worldwide economy requests versatility and ground breaking techniques from organizations to remain cutthroat and flourish. When we look ahead, there are a few key strategies that stand out as essential to success in the changing markets.

First and foremost, it is basic to embrace innovative progressions. The Fourth Modern Upheaval has introduced another time of advancement, with innovations like man-made reasoning, blockchain, and the Web of Things reshaping enterprises. To remain at the forefront of global market trends, businesses must not only adopt these technologies but also cultivate a culture of continuous learning and adaptation.

Moreover, maintainability is at this point not a choice yet a need. As natural worries rise, customers and partners progressively focus on eco-accommodating practices. Organizations that coordinate manageability into their basic beliefs add to a superior world as well as gain an upper hand on the lookout. Maintainable practices appeal to earth cognizant purchasers as well as draw in financial backers who perceive the drawn out reasonability of socially capable organizations.

Moreover, an emphasis on developing business sectors is essential for future business achievement. As customary business sectors immerse, organizations should investigate and put resources into locales with undiscovered possibility. Arising economies offer new client bases, and understanding the exceptional difficulties and open doors in these business sectors is pivotal for supported development. Laying out serious areas of strength for an in these districts from the get-go can give a critical benefit as they keep on creating.

Globalization stays a main thrust, however the way to deal with it is developing. As opposed to a one-size-fits-all system, organizations ought to embrace a limited methodology. Figuring out the subtleties of each market, including social inclinations and administrative scenes, is fundamental. Products and services that resonate with local customers are made more acceptable and successful in a variety of markets thanks to this localization strategy.

Besides, deftness is a foundation of outcome later on in the business scene. A competitive advantage is the capacity to quickly adapt to shifting market conditions, consumer preferences, and technological advancements. It is important for businesses to cultivate a culture that places a high value on adaptability and creativity, allowing them to quickly adjust to new trends and challenges.

Cooperation and organizations are additionally essential parts of future business methodologies. In a hyper-associated world, no business works in disconnection. Cooperative endeavors with different organizations, new businesses, or even contenders can prompt collaborations that drive advancement and improve market intensity. Businesses can make use of each other's strengths and work together to solve difficult global problems.

Moreover, a solid accentuation on information driven direction is fundamental. Businesses now have unprecedented access to information thanks to big data. Companies gain a competitive advantage when they use data analytics to gain useful insights. Understanding client conduct, market patterns, and interior tasks through information examination empowers informed direction and proactive reactions to showcase changes.

As we expect future worldwide business drifts, a strong network safety methodology can't be disregarded. With expanded dependence on advanced innovations, the danger scene has extended. Safeguarding delicate data and guaranteeing the uprightness of business tasks are foremost. Organizations should put resources into cutting edge network safety gauges and teach representatives on accepted procedures to alleviate dangers and construct entrust with clients.

Besides, ability securing and maintenance assume a crucial part in forming the future progress of organizations. As the business scene advances, so do the abilities expected for progress. Organizations need to put resources into persistent preparation and improvement projects to upskill their labor force and draw in top ability. Cultivating a different and comprehensive work environment isn't simply an ethical objective yet additionally an upper hand, offering alternate points of view and thoughts that might be of some value.

the fate of worldwide business requires a multi-layered approach that envelops mechanical development, maintainability, market limitation, nimbleness, cooperation, information driven direction, network protection, and ability improvement. In today's dynamic and competitive global business environment, companies that proactively implement these key strategies position themselves not only to survive but also to thrive. When we look to the future, it is abundantly clear that those who are able to navigate the complexities of the future with foresight, perseverance, and a commitment to ongoing improvement will be successful.

www.ingramcontent.com/pod-product-compliance
Lightning Source LLC
Chambersburg PA
CBHW050309230526
45471CB00005B/2100